MyriadPRESS

Welcome.

Life is your classroom.

The goal is to live it at play.

Reaching the goal will require a PhD in ME.

Make Your Life Vivid is your textbook.

Your *"thesis"* is to write your PLAYBook.

Access the resources you will need.

Visit playbook.gwenwitherspoon.com or scan the QR code to download worksheets, get video links, and other resources.

I am your instructor. *Need help?*

Let's Talk.

< Scan to Schedule

To my husband, Ron
My vivid life story began with divine design.
Now, thanks to our meeting, our art,
and our God, I can tell it to the world.

To Mommy & Daddy
God made me the first so He could make you
the best parents a girl could ever have.
My light shines brighter because of your cheers.

To Bernard & Karen
You will forever be the spiritual parents
God used to birth me into my destiny.

© 2024 by Myriad Press. All rights reserved. No part of this publication may be reproduced, distributed, or transmitted in any form or by any means, including photocopying, recording, or other electronic or mechanical methods, without the prior written permission of the publisher, except in the case of brief quotations embodied in critical reviews and certain other noncommercial uses permitted by copyright law.

Published by: Myriad Press, Post Office Box 110278, Atlanta, Georgia 30311.

For permission requests, contact: Myriad Press, Post Office Box 110278, Atlanta, Georgia 30311. Email: permissions@myriadpress.us, website: myriadpress.us

First Edition

Library of Congress Cataloging-in-Publication Data

Author: Gwen Witherspoon
Title: Make Your Life Vivid: A Guide to Understanding Who You Are, What You Have to Offer, & Your Life's Work
Publication Info: Atlanta, Georgia: Myriad Press, 2024.
ISBN: 978-1-300-99139-7

Printed in the United States of America

Cover and book design by Adam Red

Make Your Life ViViD

A GUIDE TO UNDERSTANDING WHO YOU ARE,
WHAT YOU HAVE TO OFFER, & YOUR LIFE'S WORK

GWEN WITHERSPOON

MyriadPRESS

CHAPTER ONE • [A CALL TO ADVENTURE]

Resist the Urge to Be a Copy 13

INTRODUCTION: *Is the Vivid Life for you?*

My Vivid Life Story 13
What You Can Expect From Me 15
Your Call to Adventure 17
Getting Your Head Right 19
About Brain Hacks For Productivity 20
Ready to Answer the Call to Adventure? 20
How to Use This Book 21

CHAPTER TWO • [AN INVITATION TO BE THE ARCHITECT OF YOUR FUTURE]

The Future is Yours to Create 23

VISION: *What would make your life better?*

What is vision? 23
What is a visionary? 25
Are we all visionaries? 26
Develop a Vision for Every Area of Life 28
Is it a dream, a vision, or a goal? 30
Should you get your eyes examined? 31
Make Vision Statements That Evoke Emotion 34
Every Journey Needs a Map 36
You Need Perspective: Begin With a Survey 40
Your Vivid Life Needs a PLAYBook 41
RE-VIEW: VISION, A.C.T. List, & Resources 43

Contents

CHAPTER THREE • [AN OPPORTUNITY TO BECOME THE HERO OF YOUR OWN STORY]
Hero or Villain? You Decide 47
IDENTITY: *Who do you think you are?*

Solving Your Identity Crisis 52
Love & Self Discovery 53
Defining Your Identity 54
Earning a PhD in ME 56
7 Signs It's Time to Rebrand Yourself 57
How to Create Your Identity Map 60
Seize the Opportunity 62
RE-VIEW: IDENTITY, A.C.T. List, & Resources 63

CHAPTER FOUR • [A RESPONSIBILITY TO BE THE ANSWER]
You Are God's Gift to the World 67
INFLUENCE: *What problem were you born to solve?*

Influence Matters More Than Achievement 68
Discovering Your Influence In Five Builder Types 68
Developing Your Influence Map 72
Facing & Overcoming Roadblocks 73
The Call to Be Salt & Light 74
Influence Requires Both Faith & Action 75
The Breadth of Influence: More Than Fame 75
The Price of Influence 75
The Responsibility of Influence 76
Your Influence Matters 77
RE-VIEW: INFLUENCE, A.C.T. List, & Resources 79

CHAPTER FIVE • [AN ASSIGNMENT TO CHANGE THE WORLD]
You Can Do Greater Works 83
IMPACT: *What are you called to build?*

Seeing the World & Your Role In It 85
The World Is Your Playground...87
Developing Your Impact Map...88
You Are God's Greatest Work 90
Your Personal Assignment to Impact the Nations..91
The Importance of Impact Entrepreneurship..92
Wealth Creation As An Economic Engine...93
Invest Your Life's Work to Do the Impossible...91
RE-VIEW: IMPACT, A.C.T. List, & Resources 95

CHAPTER SIX • [TOOLS TO TURN YOUR THOUGHTS INTO ACTION]
Six Brain Hacks to Command Your Day 99
PRODUCTIVITY: *What habits will shape your future?*

Developing Your Productivity Map...100
Brain Hacks to Make You More Productive...101
#1 How to Write Your Vision [VIVID Model] 102
#2 How to Plan Anything [Building the Ark]...106
#3 How to Produce [Clear the Brain Storm] 114
#4 How to Change Any Habit [REPOH] 120
#5 How to Become [WORKS Model]..122
#6 How to Live Life At Play [PLAY Formula & Model] 126
RE-VIEW: PRODUCTIVITY & Resources 130

Contents

CHAPTER SEVEN • [A DARE TO RECAPTURE YOUR CHILDLIKE WONDER]
Live Purposed, Liberated, Aligned, & Yielded 133
LIVING LIFE AT PLAY: *What's your unique PLAYBook?*

You Need a Personal Brand Guide	134
You Are a Work of Art	135
The Science of Your Creation: Wonderful & Complex	136
Understanding Your Psychology	137
Acting On What You Believe	138
You Have to Become the Prophet of Your Own Future	139
The Work of Becoming	140
The Dignity & Divinity of Work	143
Five Keys to Finding Your Purpose	145
Purpose is Liberating	147
Say Goodbye to Constraints	148
The Exhilaration of Alignment: Living True to Your Design	149
The Freedom of Yielding: Embracing Life's Flow	150
Transformation is a Team Sport	151
RE-VIEW: PLAY, A.C.T. List, & Resources	155

CHAPTER EIGHT • [TIME TO GLOW UP, SHOW UP, & GROW UP]
No More Hiding Your Light & Playing Small 159
CONCLUSION: *Are you ready to stop making excuses?*

The Art, Science, & Psychology of a Vivid Life	160
Defining Your Personal Brand With AI	162
Telling Your Vivid Life Story With Global Reach	163
Come Out of Hiding	165
Finishing Well	166
RE-VIEW: CONCLUSION, A.C.T. List, & Resources	171

About the Author	174
References	176

CHAPTER ONE • INTRODUCTION

Resist the Urge to Be a Copy
[A CALL TO ADVENTURE]

Is the Vivid Life for you?

This book is for those who know, deep down, they were meant for something more. You feel it—the nagging sense that your life is supposed to be bigger, brighter, more purposeful. Maybe you have tried to shake it off, thinking it was just a fleeting dream or that life's demands have buried it. That feeling just will not leave you. No matter how much you have accomplished, there is still a small voice inside that says, *"This isn't it. There has to be more."*

Perhaps you have questioned, *"Why do others seem to have it all together? Why can't I figure out how to turn this burning desire into something real, something tangible?"* Maybe you have achieved *success* by the world's standards, but it does not feel like what you expected. The life you are living does not fully match the person you know you are meant to be.

This book is for you—the visionary who refuses to settle, the dreamer who will not give up, the change maker who aches to make a difference. It is for those who have felt the sting of trying and failing, only to realize that the failure was not final—it was part of the process, and you still believe. It is for those who, *like me,* know that there is more to their story waiting to be written.

Let me introduce myself so you will know where I am coming from, as well as the purpose of this book. My story—*and yours*—begins in childhood. When I look back, it was so obvious that organized little girl in love with words and art was a publisher, a teacher, and a poet. Passing my weekly spelling tests in third grade meant that I consistently earned a deep dive into the Brach's candy bag.

Make Your Life Vivid

The jelly nougats were my favorite. If I close my eyes, I can still taste the sweet reward from my teacher.

My first stab at righting the wrongs of society was when I penned a guide to Barbie care. Written in crayon on construction paper and bound with staples, I am reminded of the satisfaction I felt as I passed them out to my 9-year-old girlfriends. I was confident that I had changed the world–*if only for Barbie.*

Though high school was marked by cheerleading, track, student government, choir, and the lead role in *Bye Bye Birdie,* my Yearbook and AP English classes were my happy places. That is when I learned to interpret classic literature and write poems for my eyes only.

Then, there was the college newsletter, *The Drakevine,* that I named after what we affectionately called the Black student rumor mill at Drake University. I was compelled to write it. I was coping with being away from my parents and caring that I was the *only*–both for the first time. So, I took it upon myself to keep the small group of minority students at this Iowa liberal arts school informed. My introduction to Black literature meant that I regularly included the poetry of Nikki Giovanni, Langston Hughes, and the like. I am not sure what it meant to anyone else, but I painstakingly wrote, edited, laid out, and distributed every issue as a survival mechanism.

I left Des Moines, armed with a bachelor's degree in graphic design and a minor in journalism. That education was the foundation of a forty-year career in marketing communications. Yet, it has taken all of that time to realize I was always trying to say something, to make sense of my ideas—*to matter*. More importantly, now I know *why* anyone should care about what I have to say.

I finally understand that I help visionary leaders like you tell their vivid life stories so you can live life at play—*effectively doing, while delightfully being*. The alternative is to succumb to the temptation to become a copy of someone else and miss out on all the goodness available to you.

These details are critical to *my* vivid life story. When I recall them, they stand out as evidence of who I am, what I have to offer, and my life's work. They reveal so much about what delights me now and the origins of my life at play, even today. So, what about you? *What does your childhood show you?* Does the way you live now reflect what you see? If you are ready for more, I am inviting you to step into your own adventure—*your vivid life story.*

CHAPTER 1: Introduction

I have another question for you, *"Is the Vivid Life for you?"* I ask because, if the answer is, *"Yes,"* it is something you will have to fight for over and over and over again. Once you are engaged in hardcore adulting, dreaming can feel like foolishness. Getting all the love, joy, fulfillment, purpose, and wealth you can handle takes work. However, the hardest work is on your inside world. It can be intimidating, terrifying, and debilitating to face yourself. The more committed you are to the process, the greater the reward. My life at play means that I get out of bed every day excited about becoming, and my actual dreams become marching orders when I wake up. You can do the same.

If there is even the slightest ache in your heart for what you believed about yourself as a child, this book should help. If the possibility of more beauty, pleasure, and sweetness appeals to you, you are in the right place. It would not be fair if I did not add a disclaimer: I know that what I will be asking you to do throughout this book is not easy. I also know that as I have taken the same *"medicine,"* I have emerged healed, confident, and focused. I can testify that it is worth the work.

If there is one ounce of regret, one shred of disappointment, one iota of longing when I ask these questions, this book could be exactly what you need. Just know that I will be right here with you.

What You Can Expect From Me

I am a learner. My biggest lesson from my MBA coursework came when I read a statistic in one of my textbooks. It said that only 5% of businesses succeed in the first year. What? That one statistic set me free! From that day forward, I was forever liberated from the dread of *"doing it wrong,"* *"making a mistake,"* and *"losing."* I embraced the fact that *"success"* comes by failing often and well. I have emerged as an expert.

At my core, **I am a teacher.** Binders, folders, and notebooks are my jam, and I have been known to shed a small tear over a well-designed chart. You could consider me a knowledge nerd because Word Work is my love language. When I learn something, watch out. Everybody needs to know, and I will go to great lengths to get the message across. In my world, no idea is too hard, too complex, or unknowable if it will help someone change or grow. I *must* try to explain, encourage, and support. I cannot help myself.

Improper grammar aside, **I love me some people.** My infinite belief in people draws me to an idea like a moth to a flame. Most of my life I have been sucked in with no power to resist. This quality has been a blessing and a curse. Now in my gray hair season, I hope I have gained the wisdom to put my proverbial mask on first.

I am an author. That is why I am writing this book. I have a need to use my very being to make a difference, but I cannot do that if I continue neglecting my gifts to help others develop theirs. I have to stop giving every would-be author step-by-step instructions for writing their book, when mine are never published. If this book is for you, I can see you in my mind's eye screaming, *"Yes,"* because you have felt the same way.

I am a coach. You come to me when you are ready to make your weaknesses irrelevant, find your rhythm, and receive everything God has destined for you. Your life is less about what is happening to you as it is what you think about what is happening. I like to create what I call *"brain hacks,"* so if you can think differently about what makes you stop, you will hack the triggers that cause you to judge, doubt, or give up on your ideas. Every top performer has a coach—*a team of coaches*, even. (I hope you will allow me to be one of them for you.)

I am a builder. I used to believe that entrepreneurship was only about business. In reality, building a company was really about building me. The one problem I was born to solve is Identity. It has been the thread that runs through every project, every brand, every personal interaction. I like to say entrepreneurship is helping me earn a PhD in ME.

I am an artist. My art is my life. My art is my gift (to myself and others). My art is my tool. Like a Swiss Army knife, it transforms to meet the need of the moment. I am equal parts designer, poet, and brand architect.

I am a believer. As a child of God, my faith informs my work, my ideas, and my motivation. You will see scripture references from the Bible that are the backbone of my philosophies. I share the revelations I apply practically to my life and business. (Even if you do not share this faith tradition, I hope that you will recognize timeless principles that you can apply anyway.)

All of this is evidence that I have always been that little girl in her room using what she has around her to make sense of the world by organizing, making, and building. I am still living my life at play, and I want to help you do the same.

Your Call to Adventure

My goal for writing *Make Your Life Vivid: A Guide to Understanding Who You Are, What You Have to Offer, & Your Life's Work* is to invite you back to the place of childhood wonder. My life as a builder has included direct sales, luxury retail management, church founding and ministry leadership, startups, social entrepreneurship, publishing, and more. However, my work is about people. I have always invested my time, talent, and treasure in people and their ideas–the *true wealth*, and I am obsessed with vision. This book is my investment in you and your ideas. **As you read it, will you allow me to be your coach?**

I understand the frustration of thinking big when your life feels small, the insecurity of sending your ideas into the world for judgment, and the crushing disappointment when nothing seems to be working after giving your all. Surely there was something wrong with me that had to be fixed. Maybe I needed another credential or a big client. If only I could hire a team, buy that equipment, or get funding. The common denominator was me. I was out here winging it. Alone. My hustle was strong, but I needed examples, mentors, and a guide to help me understand how to make what I saw in my head and felt in my heart happen.

So, I am pouring out the wisdom gained from my own internal battles on these pages. Just call me *"Gwenfucius."* You see, I believe that I was fearfully and wonderfully made[1] in the image and likeness of God.[2] I believe that every good and perfect gift[3] belongs to me. I believe the end of my vivid life story is good[4]– *marked by beauty, pleasure, and sweetness.*[5] I also believe that with all of that comes a responsibility to complete my assignment—*the God-breathed vision for my life*.

"Without a vision, the people perish."
Proverbs 29: 18 King James Version

When I heard what I believed was God's direction, when I received a revelation of my purpose, when I was introduced to the power of vision, I was set on fire. Sometimes it was fuel. At other times, it was consuming. Then, there were the times it felt destructive. Makes me sweat a little bit just thinking about it. Vision is a transformative force. Proverbs 29: 18 says that without it, we perish, and I know what perishing feels like. Another translation says that we need a revelation[6] of what God is doing.[7] Vision is the key to who you are, what you have to offer, and your life's work. Your Creator wants to give you a vision for every area of your life.

"Write the vision, and make it plain..."
Habakkuk 2: 2 King James Version

It is your responsibility to write the vision. Let us pause for some Word Work. In Habakkuk 2: 2, *write* comes from the Hebrew word *kathab* (pronounced *kaw-thab'*). It means *to engrave, describe, inscribe, prescribe, subscribe, record, and write up*. The word *plain* means *to dig, engrave, declare, and explain*. Whew! That tells me that writing is not a one-time occurrence. Instead, it is a process. I call that process making it V.I.V.I.D.™ It is an acronym for **Vision**, **Identity**, **Voice**, **Information**, and **Development**. Making your vision vivid is the process of writing it on paper, on your heart, and on your mind beginning with five questions. (I will tell you more about this is Chapter Six.) A vivid vision will transform your thinking, compel you to take action, and make you and your ideas irresistible–*essentially making your weaknesses irrelevant.*

"Make a careful exploration of who you are and the work you've been given, and then sink yourself into that." – Galatians 6: 4 The Message

A vivid vision begins with you. No matter what you are building, you are at the center of it. Your identity, your influence, and your impact are the heart of the positive future you imagine. Do you have a dream, but you are confused about how to put the pieces together? Do you know you need help, but you are not sure who to trust? Are you able to reconcile who you are with what you do? My goal is to get in your head and help you understand that everything you need is inside of you. When you become a student of your design, your purpose, and your destiny and step up to complete your unique assignment, your vivid life story will begin. You need a vision for every area of life, and I want to help you answer three questions in Chapters Three, Four, & Five: 1) about your identity, **Who do you think you are?**, 2) about your influence, **What problem were you born to solve?**, and 3) about your impact, **What are you called to build?** Answering these questions will help you examine yourself, your influence on your immediate surroundings, and your impact beyond the *"now."*

CHAPTER 1: **Introduction**

Simply put, your assignment is to go to work on your vision and yourself. Galatians 6: 4, 5 from The Message translation says, *"Make a careful exploration of who you are and the work you've been given, and then sink yourself into that. Don't be impressed with yourself. Don't compare yourself with others. Each of you must take responsibility for doing the creative best you can with your own life."*

"...Risk your life and get more than you ever dreamed of. Play it safe and end up holding the bag."
Luke 19: 26 The Message

You were born to produce. The Parable of the Talents in Matthew 25: 14-30 and Luke 19: 12-28 tells a story of three people entrusted with wealth. One received five bags, another received two, and the other received one. The first two doubled what they were given, while the one who received one buried what he received because of fear. When I see that his approach did not work out very well for him, it tells me that each one of us has both an opportunity and an obligation to invest our lives into work that matters.

Your wealth was embedded in you as a child. Your hopes, dreams, and ideas were a sign. Who were you then? When did you lose your childlike faith? I believe that is when your identity crisis began. Knowing who you are, what you have to offer, and your life's work will change everything. As your coach, I want to give you the tools to develop your inside world so you can change the outside world just by being yourself.

Getting Your Head Right

Though I believe you were born to produce, your productivity is not about doing more. It is about turning your thoughts into action. To live that way, you must get your head right first. Life is the biggest project you will undertake. It is intended to bring the best out of you for investment in the lives of others. What you believe about who you are and what you have to offer either limits or empowers your life's work. As your coach, my ultimate goal is to help you tell your vivid life story so you can glow up, show up, and grow up to receive everything God intended for you. That is living your life at play—*effectively doing, while delightfully being.* **Pro Tip: If you are not living your God-designed, vivid life, whatever is going on in your head is stopping you dead in your tracks.** The good news is you do not have to stay there.

About Brain Hacks for Productivity

Your brain is wired to seek safety and avoid discomfort, which can make challenges and changes feel overwhelming. When faced with obstacles, your mind will default to patterns of thinking that protect you from perceived danger, like failure, the unknown, or a loss of control.

"Hesitation, indecisiveness, and procrastination are emotional stutters." – Gwen Witherspoon, @gwenfucius

I have developed a series of brain hacks—*mental models*—that will help you break through mental barriers to get your head right. By changing how you think about problems, you can bypass the triggers that make you hesitate, doubt, or stop altogether. Hesitation, indecisiveness, and procrastination are emotional stutters. Applying these mental models—simple, practical tools to shift your perspective—you gain clarity and confidence for decisive action. I will share these easy-to-remember techniques in chapter six, giving you the practical *"how-tos"* you need to do the hard things.

1 How to Write Your Vision [VIVID Model]: Understand how to apply Habakkuk 2: 2 to write your vision and make it vivid.

2 How to Plan Anything [Building the Ark]: Do you need to build something big? Every plan needs a blueprint. Use this model to never be intimidated by the process again.

3 How to Produce [Clear the Brain Storm]: Organize the mental clutter, and learn how to master your habits.

4 How to Change Any Habit [REPOH]: Learn this principle by Alfred Hollingsworth, and trade your unproductive habits for lasting change.

5 How to Become [WORKS Model]: Use this model to understand that becoming is an action that requires work.

6 How to Live Life At Play [PLAY Formula & Model]: Live with the confidence that you are purposed, liberated, aligned, and yielded.

Ready to answer the call to adventure?

The horizon is wide open in front of you, full of possibilities and untapped potential. This is your moment—*your adventure*. It is a journey to help you

CHAPTER 1: Introduction

understand who you are, what you have to offer, and your life's work. Every challenge, every setback, and every decision, will write your story—*your vivid life story*. You get to decide if you will be the hero or the villain. I am here to help you resist the urge to be a copy of anyone else. You can recapture your childlike wonder and live your life at play: purposed, liberated, aligned, and yielded. No more dimming your light and playing small. Do you want to glow up, show up, and grow up? Let's make your life vivid!

> ## How to Use This Book
>
> *Make Your Life Vivid* is a guide. At the end of each chapter, you will find three sections to help reinforce and apply what you have learned:
>
> **Re-VIEW:** This summary offers a concise, bullet-point overview of the chapter's main ideas. It is perfect for quick reference to enable you to take another view, helping you recall key points without reading the entire chapter again. Think of it as a way to reinforce your understanding and keep essential concepts fresh in your mind.
>
> **A.C.T. List:** The acronym stands for Action to Complete This Task and serves as your personal workshop for each chapter. It includes prompts and exercises based on the chapter's core questions. Use these prompts to reflect deeply and apply each lesson to your life. By actively engaging with these questions, you will change your thoughts and increase your ability to take transformative action.
>
> **Resources:** Find tools to help you take practical steps to apply what you read. They may include worksheets available for download, additional reading, or expanded instructions that build on the chapter's content.
>
> By utilizing these sections, you can turn your thoughts into action, ensuring that each concept becomes a practical part of your vivid life. As your coach, I am here to support you every step of the journey to understand who you are [identity], what you have to offer [influence], and your life's work [impact].

CHAPTER TWO • VISION

The Future is Yours to Create

[AN INVITATION TO BE THE ARCHITECT OF YOUR FUTURE]

What would make your life better?

Have you been resisting that pull inside you—that knowing that you were meant for something more? That is the power of vision calling you into the life you were designed to live. It will not leave you alone because vision is more than a dream or a wish. It is a revelation of the future that is waiting for you. It is that abundant life waiting for you to believe it is possible. You have to dare to ask for what you want—the more impossible, the better. Asking is an act of faith. It is a spiritual key that opens the door to transformation. The wonderful thing is, you get to be an active participant in the process. You are not a victim of circumstances. What if that frustration you feel was actually there to make you uncomfortable enough to create the future you imagine?

Vision is crucial in every area of life. It serves as a compass for decision-making and goal-setting. Without it, you have no direction, no boundaries, and no hope. There is a deep dissatisfaction that comes from not having hope for the future. It could lead to isolation, depression, and even death. Feelings of frustration, regret, or even anger are not just random emotions—they are signals, urging you to uncover your deepest desires and unmet needs. They serve as signposts along the path to your God-designed future.

Vision is a living force—one that will not rest until you yield to it. Your vision should answer the pressing questions within you and serve as a roadmap for your personal and professional growth. The first step is to decide that you want the abundant, brilliant, meaningful life that is available to you. Newsflash! Answering will require the use of your dreaming muscles. I understand this may be difficult because they are possibly atrophied. Trauma, trouble, and turbulence will make dreams wither away. They are often replaced with facts, with *"reality"*. Thankfully, vision is not just a dream. I mentioned that it is a revelation that provides insight. Since I have a vision, my vivid life is based on a new reality. **My identity** is rooted in my confidence in God's love for me. **My influence** is evident the more I embrace my divine design. **My impact** is inevitable as I share what I have to offer. Vision should permeate every aspect of your life. A lack of vision in any area can cause stagnation and deterioration. *No, thank you!* I do not want that for you, so it is time to imagine your future. You need a vision that not only switches your life from grainy black and white to 4K Ultra HD but also serves as GPS to navigate your journey. Without it, you have a vision problem.

    I know firsthand how vision can transform your life. Can I take you back to explain how vision became so important me? I went through a spiritual transformation that started in the summer of 1981 right after I graduated from Bartlett-Begich High School in Anchorage, Alaska. My best friend, Jackie, and I were in a band called *Chocolate Swirl*. She was Chocolate. I was Cinnamon. The other girls were Honey and Caramel, *but I digress*. Jackie knew that I was enamored by strong vocalists. So, she used that fact to invite me to a midnight musical at Greater Friendly Temple Church of God in Christ, shortened to COGIC. I will never forget the women who stepped forward and belted out pure power without a microphone. I was hooked. Fast forward to the night I could not stop crying. It was more than the voices that echoed through that small building. I accepted an invitation to come forward for prayer. The rest, as they say, is history. I wish I could tell you a dramatic born again story, but it was pretty uneventful—except that I can look back and realize that I changed for the better from that moment.

    I was told to read my Bible and to ask the Holy Spirit for help if I did not understand something, so that is what I did. Fast forward to college in Des Moines, Iowa at Drake University and the gospel choir. For four years, the student members were my only church. Our leader, Angie, and I became friends. She came from a COGIC background too, and as I helped her, we talked about how we wished there was a systematic way to learn about God,

CHAPTER 2: **Vision**

rather than being thrown into that week's Sunday School lesson.

Now, let's jump back to my BF Jackie. Not only was she instrumental in my salvation experience, she also walked me down the aisle to rededicate my life during every college and holiday break. She was there after I returned from college, and once again, she invited me to church–*only this time, it would be the answer to my heart cry in college.* Prevailing Word Outreach Church was different. The music was strange compared to what I was used to in Baptist and Pentecostal circles. The congregation was diverse. I was not used to that in any church. What mattered most though, was the message. Bernard Smalls was teaching about vision, and that turned out to be my Paul-on-the-road-to-Damascus[8] moment. Hearing Proverbs 29:18 and that there was something bigger available to me was a life-altering encounter with the Word of God and the beginning of a complete transformation in my beliefs about myself and my life purpose. **My focus was no longer on doing the right thing but becoming everything God designed.** That is the power of vision. It can change everything, *starting with you.*

What is a visionary?

I help visionary leaders stop dreaming and start doing. If you are thinking that the term *"visionary"* does not apply to you, I want to challenge that belief. **A visionary is someone who looks to the future with imagination or wisdom.** I am going to bring you back to Proverbs 29:18 a lot. One more time, it tells us that without a revelation of what God is doing, people cast off restraint. This shows that vision is from God, and we are all responsible for discovering what He wants us to do with our lives. As John 3:16 reminds us, perishing is preventable.

A visionary looks ahead and imagines a future that others might not see. With imagination and wisdom, they develop ideas and solutions that challenge the norm. They turn their ideas into action, often pushing boundaries and opening new possibilities in how we live, work, or create. Visionaries come in many forms—thought leaders, connectors, performers, storytellers, advocates—but they all share one thing: the ability to inspire change and progress. Their sight is not limited to what is. They see what could be. Whether leading a company, writing a novel, changing a neighborhood, or designing new technology, visionaries create a future that others would deem impossible.

Visionaries are the driving force behind societal, technological, and artistic progress. They have the courage to dream bigger, push limits, and lead others toward a better future. If you have ever been inspired by someone with a clear vision of what could be—*and the passion to make it happen*—you have experienced the power of a visionary.

Visionaries have a rich imagination. They come up with bold ideas that break away from traditional thinking, often leading to significant change or advancement. Visionaries do not just think big—*they think different*. They plan for the long-term and map out the steps needed to bring their visions to life. They see the big picture but also grasp the details that make it work.

Visionaries motivate others. They communicate their vision in ways that inspire belief and action. It is not just about charisma. Visionaries connect with people and get them excited about the future.

Visionaries are the biggest losers. Making a vision vivid is not easy, and visionaries know that. They are not afraid to fail. They face challenges and setbacks but keep coming back stronger. They gain courage and strength because they believe each roadblock, each wrong turn, each detour only gets them closer.

Visionaries constantly look for new ways to improve and innovate. They are not content with the status quo and are always exploring better ways to solve problems or create something new. They embrace change and understand that any forward movement is progress. They are not waiting for perfection.

Are we all visionaries?

Being a visionary does not just apply to world-changing leaders. Usually, we think of visionaries as these extraordinary people—the ones who introduce groundbreaking ideas that make the news. If you take a broader view, being a visionary is really about imagining a better future and working toward it. In that sense, I believe the potential for visionary thinking exists within all of us. So, the term *"visionary"* applies to you. Making your life vivid means taking ownership of your personal brand and building the future you want.

Vision is part of your God-design. Every one of us should be a visionary in our own lives. Whether it is setting ambitious goals for your career, your relationships, or personal growth, you are envisioning a future that is different from where you are now. You are creating a path toward something better.

Any time you come up with a new or better way to solve a problem—*whether at work, at home, or in your community*—you are using visionary thinking. You are not just accepting things as they are. You are imagining how they could be and taking steps to get there.

Whenever you engage in a creative endeavor, you are imagining something that does not exist yet, which is a form of visionary thinking. Whether you are an artist, a writer, or an inventor, you are using the same skills as any visionary—bringing the unseen into reality.

If you are someone who speaks up for change, whether in laws, societal norms, or even in your family, you are applying visionary thinking too. You are imagining a world that is better and taking action to make it so.

Your visionary powers have to be activated. Cultivate curiosity by staying open to new ideas and experiences. The more you explore, the more your mind expands to envision different outcomes. Engage in continuous learning because the more you know, the more connections you can make, and the more possibilities you can see. So, keep learning about a wide range of topics, even those outside your usual areas of interest. Practice forward thinking by taking time to think about the future regularly. *What kind of person do you want to be? What kind of life do you want? What kind of world do you want to live in?* **Pro-tip: Reflection like this makes despair and discouragement uncomfortable.**

Surround yourself with diverse perspectives by collaborating with people from different backgrounds. This interaction will inspire new ideas and help you see the world in new ways, expanding your vision even further. Not everyone will be a visionary in the household name sense, but the ability to cultivate visionary thinking—*envisioning a better future, whether for yourself, your circle, your city, or beyond*—is something we all have. It is just a matter of recognizing it and turning it on.

Develop a Vision For Every Area of Life

Vision is the key to everything—*your inside, your outside, and your surroundings.* Vision is not optional in any area of your life. Where there is no vision, there is only drift, and that drift can lead to stagnation, aimlessness, and even despair. Vision brings every aspect of life into focus. **Vision is all about providing the solution to the problem you were put here to solve and building the future you have been destined to create.** Personally, I am great at developing a vision for a business or a solution to a problem someone brings to me. My brain goes into overdrive, and I naturally start strategizing, but I have to admit, I struggle to apply that same energy to other areas of my life. Maybe you can relate. Some people are great at creating a cozy, comfortable home environment but struggle to step forward as the center of attention. Others might excel at physical discipline and fitness but lack vision for their emotional or spiritual growth. There is always room for improvement.

Any area of life where you are not thriving is an opportunity for vision. For years, I thought I would always struggle financially, but what I learned was that I needed information and a clear vision for what I wanted my financial life to look like. Once I had that vision, I started acting in alignment with it, and everything began to change. Each of us has the potential and ability to design the life we truly want. Quite frankly, your life is your personal brand.

Your personal brand is a reflection of your understanding of who you are, what you have to offer, and your life's work. Whether you realize it or not, you already have a personal brand. It is defined by how you perceive yourself and how you show up in the world. You can decide to show up differently— *more giving, more confident, more loving*—and create the life you want. If there is any area of your life that does not align with your divine potential, it is time to get a vision for it. It is time to imagine your future. We are all made in the image of God with the ability to create, to speak things into existence just as He did. You have the ability to see a future for yourself and then create it— *speaking it into existence and acting in expectation of its manifestation.*

Many of us pray and ask God for change, for relationships, and for solutions to our problems. The truth is, He has already given us everything we need. He formed us with a purpose, and it is our job to discover that purpose and lean into it. Most of the time, what we are waiting on is actually waiting on us to take action. I want to make a suggestion. **You need to partner with the vision God has for your life by creating a PLAYBook for the future you desire.** It will serve as a storyboard of sorts for your vivid life story.

This is the perfect place for some Word Work! The definition of *"vision"* is the ability to think about or plan the future with imagination or wisdom. Imagination is the action of forming new ideas, images, or concepts that are not present to the senses. It is a function of the human mind—*something we all possess*. Vision allows you to see beyond what is currently in front of you to design a future that aligns with your highest calling.

Vision alone is not enough. You need focus. Focus is the center of interest or activity. Once you have the big picture of your vision, you have to focus your energy on specific areas of your life. What will you work on first—*inside, outside, or surroundings*? When I talk about focus, I mean centering your attention on areas like emotional intelligence, mental capacity, physical health, or cleaning out that closet. Each of these areas requires its own vision.

For example, I love watching makeover shows because they remind me how transformative it can be when people change how they look and feel about themselves. Even something as simple as improving how you dress or how you take care of your physical body can have a huge impact on how you show up in the world. **The glow up matters.** The same is true for your surroundings. Whether it is your home, your office, or even your relationships, having a vision for your environment is essential to making your life vivid. You will get to having a vision for every area of life by focusing on one area at a time.

After vision and focus, your personal brand needs a plan. A plan is a detailed proposal for doing. It is your guide for making your vision a reality. It does not have to be rigid or overwhelming. Think of it as a flexible roadmap that helps you move forward, step-by-step. *"Flexible"* is the keyword, because inevitably, the plans we make do not work out the way we expect. *Having* a plan will provide you with the structure to adjust and keep moving as the unexpected arises. The truth is success is built on a firm, deep foundation of failure. Every failure teaches you something new and makes you stronger for the next attempt. Investors often prefer to work with someone who has failed before because they know that person has learned valuable lessons. So, if you feel like you are failing in any area of life, understand that it is a necessary step on the path to success. You are on the right track.

To summarize, developing a personal brand vision for every area of life requires three things: *imagination, focus,* and *a plan.* Imagination allows you to see the future you want to create. Focus centers your energy and attention on the specific areas you want to improve. A plan provides a guide for making that future a reality. Use all three, and you will be on your way to developing a vision for ever area of life.

Is it a dream, a vision, or a goal?

Before we go too far, **it is important to understand the distinctions between a dream, a vision, and a goal.** A dream is a broad, inspirational idea that gives you hope. It is the initial spark, the imaginative idea of what could be. It does not need a plan or structure. It just fills you with excitement and hope. Dreaming is about possibility.

A vision, however, is much more focused. It is a clear, strategic image of the future that guides your actions. **Dreams inspire us, but vision guides us.** Vision translates the intangible into a roadmap—a plan—a set of coordinates to follow. A vision without a plan is just a wish. Your plan gives shape to your vision and helps you move from dreaming to doing, one meaningful step at a time. It is a picture of where you are going and why you are going there, something you can work toward with intention. Vision is what keeps you grounded and on course when challenges arise. It helps you endure, keeping your eyes fixed on the bigger picture, and imposes discipline that allows you to make calculated decisions.

Finally, a goal is the most practical part of the equation—a measurable, time-bound objective. It is actionable, something you can work on right now. **Goals are the steps you take to bring your vision to life, the concrete actions that slowly close your wisdom gap—***the space between where you are now and where you want to be.* You need all three in your vivid life. Dreams are the raw material for vision. Vision provides direction. Goals are necessary to bring the vision to pass, but if you focus solely on short-term goals, you might find yourself busy but not fulfilled.

Vision ensures that everything you do aligns with a bigger purpose. You need a vision to navigate the wisdom gap. **No vision? You are just setting goals without knowing if they are leading you in the right direction.** Remember this: *dreams inspire you, visions guide you, and goals help you measure your progress.* Understanding how these three elements work together is key to telling your vivid life story.

Should you get your eyes examined?

Let me take you back to where all this vivid stuff came from. I have been talking about it for so long now that sometimes I forget what things were like before I started talking about it like a broken record. I have had a vision for my own agency since the nineties after my first advertising agency job right out of college. My agency has gone through three different names as I have grown on the path to becoming. The vision has evolved with me. However, there was a period where it felt like that vision was dead. There is no way to describe that season other than *"utter darkness."* I had no energy for and no interest in the dream that once consumed me. It felt like it was not going to happen, and I actually believed that my days as an entrepreneur were over.

This shift happened around the time my son graduated from high school. It was a huge transition for me, and I went through a lot of personal trauma in my first marriage. I convinced myself that I was done with entrepreneurship and was fine with just having a regular job. For 10 years, I worked in luxury retail management. I was shocked by how much I enjoyed the work. It felt as close to being an entrepreneur as I could get within a job, and for a while, I thought, *"This is it. I'm going to be here forever."* Even though I thought it had nothing to do with my entrepreneurial vision, it turned out to be one of the best experiences I could have had to prepare me for going back into business.

During that time, I felt like my entrepreneurial spirit had died. I was lost. I thought the part of me that loved building and creating was gone for good. It did not matter how long I had nurtured the vision, I just did not have the energy to pursue it. Then, something unexpected happened. While I was still in my management role, a colleague approached me for help with a new business he was starting with friends. That conversation ignited something in me. It resurrected my business vision. I renamed my business and started offering coaching and marketing services—specifically helping visionaries interpret their dreams and then providing the services they needed to make them work. **That is when I came up with the first brain hack, the V.I.V.I.D.™ Model.**

    I kept coming back to Proverbs 29: 18, which says, *"Where there is no vision, the people perish,"* and Habakkuk 2: 2, *"Write the vision and make it plain."* I heard those verses so many times, but during this period of rebirth for my business, they stood out to me in a new way. Talk about *"no vision,"* it seemed that I had gone blind, and I realized that making it plain is not just about writing it down once and thinking, *"Okay, I've done it."* No, making it plain is about repetition—*writing it, speaking it, practicing it, until it becomes a habit, until it is second nature.* Just as faith comes by hearing and hearing and hearing,[9] making your vision plain comes through constant action. V.I.V.I.D.™ is an acronym for Vision, Identity, Voice, Information, and Development, and it is all about taking your vision through that process to make it vivid. Thankfully, that dark time is a distant memory, and living life at play has become a way of life.

    There was another time when I realized I needed to have my eyes examined. Remember the pandemic? As we came to the end of 2020, I found myself asking, *"What has 2020 done to your vision?"* It is understandable if you were shaken and incredible if you rose to every challenge. No matter what, 2020 forced us all to reckon with our visions. Everywhere we turned, there was disruption. For me, I pulled out all my old notes, and with the encouragement of my colleague, my coach, and my friend Katrina Mitchell, I decided to execute the vision I had been nurturing for a live broadcast show. I had this vision back in 2015 when Facebook launched Facebook Live. I saw an ad for broadcast-quality live production and immediately thought, *"I want to do that."* I nurtured that vision for two years before deciding in 2017 to finally act on it. I hesitated because I thought, *"I cannot do this alone. I don't know how to film, how to handle the audio. I don't have the resources."* So, I shelved the idea—*for three more years*.

    Once I finally decided to launch *Vivid Talk*™ *LIVE*, I recognized that fear had been holding me back. It was so deep-seated, I was not aware that it had become my companion. It took the first few days of going live for me to break through that fear. By day three, I felt a shift. Suddenly, it became fun. The challenges—*technical issues, mistakes*—became part of the learning process.

CHAPTER 2: **Vision**

Each step forward taught me more about myself, and even though the show was very imperfect, I knew I was moving in the right direction.

I am sharing these stories because I want you to understand that vision takes time, and you will need to make adjustments to accommodate the changes in how you are viewing the twists and turns. Habakkuk 2: 3 says, *"Though the vision tarry, wait for it..."* You may feel like it is taking forever, like you will never get there, but the promise is that your vision is never late. It is not behind schedule. If the vision is divinely inspired—*if it comes from a higher source*—it will not let you go, no matter how much time passes or how discouraged you feel. I learned this lesson firsthand.

The upheavals in my life have shaken me to remind me that my vision is not just an opportunity—*it is an assignment*. So, **whatever your vision is, I want to encourage you to step forward, even if you do not feel completely prepared**. Do not wait for everything to be *"just right"*. I have learned that the obstacles you think will stop you often disappear once you start moving toward your goal. You may think you need more resources, more money, or more people, but often those solutions come after you take the first step. I am living proof of that. What I thought would require a big production crew was handled by me and my photographer husband, Ron. He dealt with the recording and gave me feedback on sound, but I ran the whole show myself. Now that I have over forty episodes under my belt, I can even do his job if I have to. The point is, you may not have everything you need right now, but God has a way of bringing things together when you start moving.

There are so many issues that could be holding you back. You will have to ask yourself, *"Is it time to get my eyes examined?"* Vision is not just the ability to physically see. It is also the ability to think about or plan the future with imagination or wisdom. If you are feeling overwhelmed, disconnected from family and friends, distracted by chaos, or just discouraged. You need to have your eyes examined for these four common vision problems: *nearsightedness, farsightedness, double vision, or blindness*. I am giddy about this analogy!

When you are so focused on immediate challenges that the bigger picture fades from view, you are **nearsighted**. Take a breath, clear out the noise, and regain focus on what is ahead. On the other hand, if you are **farsighted**, that can lead you to chase future goals while missing the precious moments right in front of you. Are you recognizing the progress you are making right now? Are you celebrating the small victories and taking time to rest? **Double vision** happens when competing ideas pull you in conflicting directions, creating confusion. The last vision problem is **blindness**. This is when your vision has lost all its color and gone dark. That will make you feel utterly discouraged, unable to see your own impact or potential.

I believe you can treat these vision problems by adjusting your thoughts, habits, and beliefs, and addressing any trauma that might be affecting your vision. **Like your physical eyesight, your vision for life is controlled by your brain, and that means your thinking plays a huge role in how clearly you see your future.** You have to train your mind, create healthy habits, and adjust your outlook to make your life vivid.

So, how do you treat vision problems? First, **change your lens**. Just like I wear glasses to help me see clearly, you may need to find new tools or perspectives to sharpen your vision. Then, if the situation is serious enough, you may need to **perform surgery**—take drastic action to remove obstacles, lies, or negative patterns that are holding you back. Finally, **adjust your lifestyle**. A healthy vision needs the right environment to grow. That means nourishment, refreshing, and time. No matter what any major disruption does to your vision, you can move forward with more clarity, more focus, and a vivid life. That is not just a motivational message—it is reality. **When addressing common vision problems, focus on taking actionable steps and holding yourself accountable.** Ask yourself what would truly enhance the quality of your life, beyond superficial desires. I am here to help you identify your deepest needs and desires, translating them into your unique PLAYBook that will propel you toward meaningful action and, ultimately, a fulfilling, vivid life.

Make Vision Statements That Evoke Emotion

When my niece, Adara, was very young, my sister took her to get an eye exam. She needed glasses. I will never forget the day that I went with them to pick up her new specs. Not even school age, she was very quiet. As my sister and I headed for the door, Adarable lingered behind not making a sound. When asked what she was doing, she gleefully responded, *"I'm seeing!"* Her delight was palpable, and I giggle every time I think about that moment even

CHAPTER 2: Vision

now that she is a whole adult. You need to be able to describe your vision in a way that evokes emotion. Everyone who hears your vivid life story will be marked by it.

Your story begins with your vision. Then, I recommend creating a series of vision statements. I suggest making five to seven points that begin with action words and make the case for your vision. The goal is to get a visceral response. You want to appeal to the inside, not just the intellect. Your first target audience is you. **Your vision has to become so vivid in you that you cannot resist pursuing it.** When that happens, you and your vision will become irresistible to the people whose frequency is tuned to your voice.

Think of this process like planning a road trip—**your vision statements describe the ultimate destination, the place you dream of reaching. It tells you, and everyone around you, where you are headed**. The purpose is to motivate and guide, keeping you, your spouse, your family, your team, or your audience focused on moving toward that big goal, no matter how distant it may seem. For me, vision statements should go beyond just describing a goal. They should create an image of the future that stirs emotion and resonates deeply with the core of the problem you were born to solve. Vision statements that evoke strong emotions bring the future to life in a way that is aspirational, yet still feels real and tangible. They are more than just words on a page—they are a transformative experience. How does that feel? Here is an example of the vision statements for my coaching vision:

I help visionary leaders tell their vivid life stories and resist the urge to become a copy of someone else. As an artist and entrepreneur, I use art, technology, and music to define your identity, influence, and impact using my V.I.V.I.D.™ Model. I am the one you come to when you are ready to make your weaknesses irrelevant, find your rhythm, and receive everything God has destined for you.

- Create the positive future free from the problem you were born to solve.
- Glow up with unapologetic acceptance of who you are.
- Show up with unshakable confidence in what you have to offer.
- Grow up with unstoppable determination to finish your life's work.
- Make a difference by turning your thoughts into action.

These five vision statements reflect who I am, what I have to offer, and my life's work, and they are also my vision for you. This is what I want you to get from this book. By evoking emotion, your vision becomes more than just an abstract goal. It becomes something people can personally connect with, making the future feel within reach and worth striving for. Suddenly, you will have an Adara moment—*when the world suddenly comes into view.*

Every Journey Needs a Map

Imagine for a moment that you are standing at the beginning of a journey—a long road stretches ahead of you. It leads to a life filled with opportunity, challenges, and potential destinations. What do you need to successfully navigate that journey? Let me suggest something a little different. To navigate this journey, you will need a map, but not just any map. Consider writing a PLAYBook. As your coach, I will help you through the process. You need a series of maps for your life. I call them your personal brand maps. There are four of them, but let's start with the first three: identity, influence, and impact. They will help you understand who you are, what you have to offer, and your life's work. The fourth is your productivity map that defines the *"how."* They will provide a foundation for what you will need on the journey, and we are going to put it all in your PLAYBook that I will define more later.

In the same way that a physical map helps you navigate unfamiliar terrain, your personal brand maps will help you define your identity, influence, impact, and productivity as you work to make your vision vivid. Using the analogy of a physical map, let me break down why you need personal brand maps.

A Map Has a Title: Think of the title as the overarching theme of your life's journey. This is your vision—the big picture, the future you want to create. Where are you headed? So, before you even begin the journey, you need to name your vision. What do you want your life to be about? What would make your life better?

A Map Has Direction: Like a compass, your vision gives you direction. It helps you navigate decisions, large and small, keeping you focused on your true north. When challenges arise, or when opportunities present themselves, your vision is the guide that tells you which direction to go in. Without direction, you could easily get lost, wandering through life.

CHAPTER 2: Vision

What happens when you try to make important life decisions without a sense of direction? It is too easy to be thrown off trying to please others or chasing after goals that do not align with who you are. Your personal brand maps keep you on track, reminding you of your unique characteristics, contributions, and competence.

A Map Has Layers: Just as a physical map shows layers—like roads, topography, and boundaries—your personal brand maps have layers, too. These layers represent the different aspects of your life: your identity, your influence, your impact, and your productivity. Your personality, gifts, and capacity make you unique. Your maps will help you see how all these layers work together, creating a full picture of your vivid life.

A Map Has a Legend: The legend on a map explains the symbols, colors, and markings that help you read it accurately. Your personal brand maps also need a legend, but instead of geographical symbols, your legend includes the key elements of your intentions, goals, values, and experiences. These symbols help you understand what matters most to you and how to navigate your path.

For example, maybe one symbol in your legend represents your core values, like integrity or creativity. Another symbol might represent your key relationships or the communities you are called to serve. The legend of your map will help you understand the complexities of your divine design.

A Map Shows Distance and Scale: Maps are not just about where you are. They are about where you are going. Distance and scale help you understand how far you have come and how much further you have to go. Your personal brand maps illustrate your goals and timelines. Getting a sense of the scale of your journey allows you to break it down into manageable steps and keep track of your progress. If you think of your life as a series of projects—each project bringing your vision into focus—your maps help you see the bigger picture in the context of your current position.

A Map Has Labels: Finally, maps are filled with labels that mark key points along the way—cities, roads, landmarks. Labels on your personal brand maps designate your milestones and achievements. They are the checkpoints that show you are making progress, even when the journey feels long. What are the milestones you need to hit along the way to your vision? What are the moments that will let you know you are on the right track? It is so easy to feel like you are not making progress. Labeling your key milestones—*both big and small*—allows you to look back and see how far you have come. That will inspire you to keep going.

Just as you would not set out on a long road trip without a map or GPS, you should not approach your life without your personal brand maps. Having a map gives you a sense of direction, helping you navigate the challenges and opportunities that arise along the way. It shows you where you have been, where you are going, and how to get there.

Your personal brand maps answer these three key questions:

Who do you think you are?

What problem were you born to solve?

What are you called to build?

They also lay the foundation for how you will reach your destination.

As the *Queen of Charts*, I have designed four worksheets and the Flip Productivity™ Life & Action Planning System to help you. (Pro-Tip: You will find a link to download the worksheets at the end of this chapter.)

Let's take a look at the first three maps:

Identity Map | This map helps you understand who you are. It includes dimensions like your thinking pattern, behavioral style, fears, motivations, strengths, values, and calling. Knowing your identity is the foundation for everything you build because it informs your decision-making, behavior, and overall approach.

Influence Map | This map defines how you affect your immediate surroundings and the people you interact with. It helps you identify the message you want to communicate, the roles you play in groups, and the point of influence you have on others. By developing your Influence Map, you will gain insight into what others can expect from you and refine the way you inspire change in your relationships, profession, and community.

Impact Map | This map reveals how you bring value and make a lasting difference. It highlights your world view, tribe, territory, and the innovations or solutions you can provide to solve problems. It also includes outcomes like wealth (in seven dimensions), community (social, professional, educational), and your ultimate legacy. Your Impact Map is the broadest view of your life, focusing on the difference you aim to make in the world with your life's work.

The fourth map is critical because it will inform how you go about your journey:

Productivity Map | This map outlines your mission, vision, values, and the habits you need to master to achieve your goals. It serves as a guide to turn your thoughts into action. It ensures that your efforts are concentrated on an understanding of what you are setting out to do, why it matters, and how you go about it. (Pro Tip: There is a productivity map worksheet in your Flip Book.)

The Maps In Practice

When using your Identity Map, you will be able to explore your values and strengths to make sure you are working in a way that aligns with your core beliefs.

If you are struggling with how to communicate effectively with others, your Influence Map will help you assess the message you are sending, the roles you take in groups, and how others perceive you.

When it comes to leaving a lasting legacy, your Impact Map will show you how your influence and innovations are making a difference.

Finally, your Productivity Map will help you ensure that your daily habits, time management, and priorities are helping you achieve your long-term goals.

Each map serves as a reference point that allows you to navigate the complexities of who you are, what you have to offer, and your life's work. Think of them as tools that help you close the wisdom gap—the space between your current reality and the future you envision for yourself. Plotting your identity, influence, impact, and productivity will help you meet every challenge head-on, making you unapologetic, unshakable, and unstoppable.

You Need Perspective: Begin With a Survey

Just as a physical map requires a careful survey of the land, your personal brand map begins with a survey of yourself. Like a surveyor carefully setting reference points and boundaries for new construction, the process of self-discovery lays the groundwork for building a life of purpose and direction. Without an accurate understanding of who you are—your strengths, personality, thinking patterns, and vision—it is easy to drift off course, following paths that could make you feel disconnected and uncertain.

Tools for personal introspection, like personality assessments, act as survey instruments that reveal your unique landscape. They offer you insight into your design—your natural tendencies, ways of thinking, and patterns of behavior. Assessments like StrengthsFinder, BrainMap®, and Gallup's Builder Profile provide clues about the qualities that set you apart. These tools help you define the *"terrain"* of your personality, showing both your high and low points. Just as a surveyor's map reveals obstacles and opportunities in the land, personal introspection uncovers areas of strength, places for growth, and potential pitfalls.

The information you gain from these assessments also serve as markers on your map, guiding you through the diverse landscape of your life. They bring perspective to situations that might otherwise leave you feeling lost or scattered, giving you what you need to make necessary adjustments. This kind of self-awareness is essential for charting a course that feels genuine based on what drives you, what drains you, and what propels you.

When you have a detailed survey of who you are, you are equipped to make decisions that bring your identity, influence, and impact together in the most beautiful way. Ultimately, this survey is the first step toward living your life at play—*effectively doing, while delightfully being*. It lays the groundwork for crafting your personal brand maps and gives you the confidence to know that every choice, challenge, and change is part of the vivid life story that you are writing. Your personal brand maps are the core of your PLAYBook. Identity, influence, impact, and productivity shape your vivid life. Each map represents a unique aspect of how you show up. That said, I understand that I am not talking about an easy process. I realize that it is much easier to stay busy doing anything other than this deep, inside work, but it is worth it.

CHAPTER 2: **Vision**

Your Vivid Life Needs a PLAYBook

Let me take off my coach hat for a moment and put on my branding agency owner hat. Part of my vivid life story is that I was born to solve the problem of identity. There is a lot of evidence. As a graphic designer, I especially loved corporate identity. The first time I dipped my toe into entrepreneurship was as an image consultant with a direct sales cosmetics company. Doing color analysis based on the color theory I was studying in my design classes and helping clients build wardrobes inspired by their fashion personalities was too thrilling to bear. Creating branded niche publications sends me over the edge with glee. Coaching entrepreneurs, executives, and faith leaders to interpret their personal visions and then translate that into brand concepts is like breathing. After starting my career at an advertising agency, my vision to have my own was crystallized when I discovered that a *"branding"* agency was a thing. What? Talk about an epiphany. That just brought it all together. Picture me running wildly toward my destiny, arms outstretched–face covered in happy tears (and snot...tee, hee, hee). Do you see it? That was me–*ecstatic* about the birth of Adam Red.

I help visionary leaders build brands that tell stories and create experiences to inspire change, transform culture, and enrich lives. As the founder of Adam Red, I am equal parts artist and strategist, and I am the only strategic partner you need to make your vision vivid. The future you imagine is necessary to make it through the coming storm. There is a problem only you can solve, and you partner with me and my branding agency when you are ready to build a brand, not just a business.

Brands are not just for companies. You are a brand. Your vivid life is a brand waiting to be built. That is where the idea to help you create a PLAYBook came from. You need a PLAYBook so you can live purposed, liberated, aligned, and yielded. I have dreamed of sending my clients a custom magazine all about them and their vision once we finished engineering their corporate DNA. The framework I have created for my agency clients is so comprehensive that it would paint an extraordinary picture. Do you want one? Well, *Make Your Life Vivid* will give you a jump start.

Your PLAYBook is a blend of intention, reflection, and direction—equal parts journal, vision board, and scrapbook with structure and spontaneity.

Think of it as a dynamic personal brand guide. Developing it will probably feel like therapy. (That is why Adam Red's slogan is *"Your brand therapy begins now."*™ That makes me giggle.) It legitimately describes the process, and it is not for lightweights. You have to be willing to bravely step into the Light, unafraid of being scrutinized and doing the work to find your deepest desires, needs, and potential.

Consider how athletes, performers, and even businesses use playbooks. For a football team, a playbook holds the strategic moves, patterns, and plays that guide them toward victory. It does not just define *"what"* to do. It helps them anticipate challenges and adapt with flexibility. For performers, a script or choreography maps out their role while leaving room for their unique expression. In business, a playbook might capture protocols or brand guidelines to define the *"why"* and *"how"* behind each action to keep the organization's mission clear. In each scenario, a playbook is not a static set of instructions but a living document that responds to changing demands, environments, and conditions. Your PLAYBook is similar, but with a personal twist. It contains your personal brand maps. It defines your boundaries, encourages exploration, and documents your growth.

This is your formal invitation to become the architect of your future because it is yours to create. That means taking an active, intentional role in designing the life you want to lead–*your vivid life*. You have to believe in your dreams, your ideas, and your potential. As the architect, you are not passively waiting for circumstances to dictate your path. Instead, you are planning, adjusting, and building toward a vision that is uniquely yours. You will need the imagination and courage to see beyond your limitations.

Being the architect of your future requires adaptability. The plans may shift, but your commitment to creating the future must remain steady. This is a process of continual refinement, where you take stock of what you have built along the way, learn from mistakes, and revise your approach to ensure the structure remains sound. Ultimately, to be the architect of your future is to take full ownership of your life to make it vivid.

What is your vision for each area of your life? Do not leave anything unexamined or unloved. Create the future you desire by writing it down, and committing to the work. The future is truly yours to create.

CHAPTER 2: **Vision**

Re-VIEW [Vision Key Points Summary]

- Vision is a powerful call to step into the life you were designed to live.
- Vision is a living force that will not rest until you respond.
- Vision is essential for every area of life. Without it, you can drift into stagnation, frustration, and even despair.
- Your frustrations and desires are key Indicators that lead you to the future you are destined to create.
- Know the difference between a dream, a vision, and a goal. Dreams inspire, visions guide, and goals help you measure your progress.
- Proverbs 29: 18 teaches us that vision is from God and is essential for personal and spiritual well-being.

  Common Vision Problems:

  Nearsightedness – focusing only on immediate issues while losing sight of the big picture

  Farsightedness – focusing too much on the future without appreciating the present

  Double Vision – allowing competing ideas to create confusion

  Blindness – your vision loses its color, turning dark and leaving you feeling discouraged and unable to see

- Making your vision plain is not a one-time act—it is an ongoing process of writing on paper, on your heart, and on your mind.
- Brands are not just for companies. You are a brand, and your vivid life is a brand waiting to be built.
- You need a PLAYBook that is a blend of intention, reflection, and direction—equal parts journal, vision board, and scrapbook with structure and spontaneity. It includes your personal brand maps: identity, influence, impact, and productivity.

Your A.C.T. List [Action to Complete This Task]

☐ **Create a title for your PLAYBook.** | *Where are you headed?*

Your Vivid Life PLAYBook is a guide to the future you want to create. Choose a title that inspires you. Think big! This is your vivid life story.

_____

_____

_____

☐ **Answer these three key questions:**

Reflect on these questions, journaling your honest responses. Let them guide you in defining your identity, understanding your purpose, and clarifying your outcomes. These foundational answers will help you see the big picture and align your vision with your unique design.

Who do you think you are?

_____

What problem were you born to solve?

_____

What are you called to build?

_____

☐ **Take an assessment.**

Complete a personality assessment, or revisit one you have already taken Reflect on the results, taking note of words and phrases that resonate.

CHAPTER 2: **Vision**

Resources

Flip Productivity™ Flip Book Discbound Planner

Flip Productivity™ is a life and action planning system to help you plan your work, produce what you have planned, and spend more time at play. Its core product is the Flip Book discbound printed planner that is a flexible, customizable, double-sided journaling and time-tracking tool to make your vision vivid. *Start with the Plan side. Flip it over, and you're ready to Produce.*

Visit flipproductivity.com to shop planners & Power Tools

The Vivid Channel | Inspiration On Demand

Get insight into how to start, scale, and thrive in business–*and in life*–in spite of fear, pressure, and failure with *Vivid Talk™ LIVE, Vivid Talk™ Radio,* and *Vivid Magazine.*

Visit vivid.academy/channel

Recommended Assessments

- **StrengthsFinder 2.0 Online Assessment** – Identify your top 5 strengths, and make your weaknesses irrelevant.

- **BrainMap® Online Assessment** – Explore your unique thinking patterns and behavioral style.

- **Gallup's Builder Profile** – Understand your potential as a builder and leader.

Visit gwenwitherspoon.com/shop

PLAYBook Toolkit

Visit playbook.gwenwitherspoon.com or scan the QR code to download worksheets, get video links, and other resources.

CHAPTER THREE • IDENTITY

Hero or Villain? You Decide.

[AN OPPORTUNITY TO BECOME THE HERO OF YOUR OWN STORY]

Who do you think you are?

Many of us struggle with this question. We are bombarded with images of so-called *"perfection"* in the media. Our families have expectations they want us to meet. It is also too easy to allow admiration to become comparison. What if you could rewrite the script? Think of yourself as the hero in your own story, embarking on a journey toward self-discovery and fulfillment. Like any hero, you will encounter challenges and setbacks, both external and internal. These obstacles are part of what makes the journey worthwhile—they shape you, refine you, and ultimately *prepare you*. The battle to establish your identity comes from reconciling external expectations with your internal convictions. I think I have discovered the secret to winning this battle.

There are revelatory moments in my life that have marked me. One of the most consequential was hearing Myles Munroe teach from Genesis. He shared that when God wanted to create fish, He spoke to water. When He wanted to create birds, He spoke to the air. When He wanted to create mankind, He spoke to **himself**. That still makes me tear up. *"Let Us make man in Our image, according to Our likeness..."* – Genesis 1: 26 New King James Version. Verse 27 goes on, *"So God created man in His own image; in the image of God He created him; male and female He created them."*

When I heard that, something in me exploded. I realized that my origin was not just an accident of birth, nor was my identity defined merely by my family, society, or my status. In that moment, I saw that my identity was rooted in something eternal. That changed everything. **You and I were created in the image of God. That is the foundation of identity.** Just as I am Claude's first, I am my heavenly Father's daughter. I carry His image, His DNA, and His nature.

Identity refers to the distinct characteristics, qualities, and beliefs that define who we are. It encompasses a wide range of factors—*nationality, ethnicity, religion, gender, profession, hobbies, and social roles*. These aspects come together to form our unique self-concept. Identity is not fixed. It is dynamic, continuously evolving as we grow and change. It is shaped by personal choices, experiences, and external influences like culture, society, and family. The one constant is our spiritual identity. **God's design and purpose does not change, but it is up to us to discover and pursue it.** All of the elements of your identity serve your destiny. What you believe and say about you is the basis for how you exist in this world, but what your Creator believes and says about you is the basis for your vivid life. Identity is the lens through which we view the world, and more importantly, through which we view ourselves. Without clarity on who we are, it is impossible to fully embrace the vision God has for us.

"Make a careful exploration of who you are..."
Galatians 6: 4 The Message

My V.I.V.I.D.™ Model is Brain Hack #1, and I will go into more detail later, but the first step in the model is Clarify your Vision, which we covered in the last chapter. The second step is: **Establish your identity**. The key question here is, *Who do you think you are?* Galatians 6: 4-5 from The Message translation says it perfectly: *"Make a careful exploration of who you are and the work you've been given, and then sink yourself into that. Don't be impressed with yourself. Don't compare yourself with others. Each of you must take responsibility for doing the creative best you can with your own life."*

The foundation of your vivid life is knowing who you are. Since you did not make yourself, you have to launch an investigation to understand the beauty, pleasure, and sweetness of your divine birth. You may have noticed that I use that phrase a lot. Those three words represent my favorite definition of the word *"good."* Genesis 1: 31, *"Then God saw everything that He had made, and*

CHAPTER 3: Identity

indeed it was very good..." I did the Word Work a long time ago. The Hebrew word *"tob"* (pronounced *tobe*) is an adjective, a noun, and an adverb, both masculine and feminine, singular and plural. (I love how that covers it all!) In addition to *beautiful, pleasant,* and *sweet,* the word *good* also means *joyful, merry, prosperous, precious, wealthy, favored, better, glad, fine, loving, cheerful, bountiful,* and *best.* That is how God feels about you and me. Anything other than that is a misunderstanding. **You have a misunderstanding with yourself if the words that come out of your mouth about you are contrary to how you were conceived.**

Remember what it says in Galatians 6: 5? *"...Don't be impressed with yourself. Don't compare yourself with others..."* If you believe that you are superior, you have a misunderstanding. If you feel you do not measure up, you have a misunderstanding. Both attitudes are rooted in comparison, the symptom of an identity crisis. We all want to know where we came from and where we belong, but it is easy to get lost when our focus is on other people.

Comparison is the villain in the background, always tempting you to measure yourself against others. The more you compare, the further you stray from the person you were designed to be. The inner villain thrives on self-doubt and insecurity, whispering that you are either too much or not enough. As the hero of your story, your job is to quiet those voices and remind yourself that your journey is uniquely yours. You are neither superior nor inferior—*you are simply on a path that only you can walk.*

I have been a Christian since 1981. My identity changed immediately to the household of faith, and that took precedence over my natural heritage. However, I can look back now and realize that was also when the internal war over my identity began. My parents were born and raised in Mississippi. My father was in the Army, so I grew up on military bases around the country. Those environments provided some shelter from the outside world. I was educated, but I was also oblivious to history. I mentioned in the beginning that attending Drake University was the first time I cared that I was the *only*. I meant that it was not uncommon for me to be one of the few, or the only Black person, doing whatever I was interested in. It was actually normal–*until I went to Iowa.* Admittedly, I think it was more about my new spiritual identity and the milestone of moving away from my parents than the city itself. However, the culture shift was certainly part of the trifecta.

Make Your Life Vivid

My public school education did not include Black authors. I heard about slavery, but that was over. I knew about the Civil Rights Movement, but that was a long time ago. When I moved to Georgia in the late nineties, I was blown away by the realization that my parents lived in the South when there were Whites Only and Colored Only signs everywhere. The fact that they are still alive brought it very close. Imagine what it felt like to see that every generation of my family's birth certificates had a different racial designation. My parents were colored. Mine was Negro. My siblings were black. My son was African American. That is a lot to take in. My husband's San Francisco upbringing was incredibly diverse. His kindergarten class picture looked like the United Nations, and his understanding of history is quite different. Living with him has been a crash course and a pretty rude awakening.

Somewhere in there, I took a DNA test. Coincidentally, the week before I received my results, I saw a 15-minute YouTube video summarizing the Transatlantic Slave Trade. Being *high yellow* or *redbone,* as people with my complexion are called in the South, it was evident that there were European ancestors in my lineage somewhere. Knowing that and literally seeing the path of the Transatlantic Slave Trade outlined in my DNA are two very different realities. It was even more startling when I was connected to *"DNA relatives"* and saw over and over and over again cousins with 99% European ancestry. It was a lot. Add to all of these revelations what I learned about the role of Christianity in slavery and the use of the Bible while witnessing the weaponization of both in politics, it was all hard to take. I came to a crossroad. Should I continue disregarding my natural heritage in exchange for my spiritual identity? Should I renounce my Christian faith in light of the facts and questions regarding my racial and ethnic heritage?

Reconciling my spiritual identity with my natural heritage was not an easy task, but I came to realize that none of it was a mistake. I was exactly who God intended me to be—every part of my DNA was designed for His purpose. **The conclusion I have come to is this–everything I am was designed and destined by God.** None of it has taken Him by surprise, and He has a purpose for it all. He wants to use my identity *for good*. He wants to use who I am to turn the horror of my natural history into beauty. I believe He wants to use the agony of what human beings can do to each other to bring pleasure through what I have to offer. I am convinced that he wants to replace the bitterness of

CHAPTER 3: Identity

the past with the sweetness of work inspired by love.

I am 68.3% Sub-Saharan African and 30.4% European. Racially, I am comfortable being called Black or African American. Ethnically, I am primarily Nigerian, British, and Irish. Culturally, I have Southern roots. My nationality is American. My spiritual heritage is heir to the Kingdom of God. I am a female capable of greatness marked by my Creator's love for me. I embrace it all. Who am I to question how I was made? There are many nations in my DNA, and as a daughter of God, I am called to them all. I no longer question my ministry call because somebody told me I was the wrong gender. I have removed the blinders and rose-colored glasses covering the ugliness of the global condition. I am healed from the traumas of my past—*those that I caused as well as the ones that were inflicted upon me.* **I am fed. I am forgiven. I am free.**

I have an assignment to complete. Now that I know who I am, I recognize that I have everything I need, including the Spirit of God within me as my teacher, comforter, and friend. I have been given much, and much is required of me. My self-awareness is not only essential but also a responsibility. **Like me, you are the central character in your vision, and it is up to you to define and embrace who you are.** Every one of us has parts of our identity that may seem contradictory or hard to reconcile. However, once you understand that your identity is by divine design, those contradictions become part of the many plot lines of your vivid life story.

As you establish your identity, you are building the most essential foundation of your personal brand. This foundation will influence how you connect with others and the impact you are destined to have in the world. Identity is both the root and the framework, a grounding element that informs every action you will take. When you embrace your true self, you are not only acknowledging your own worth. You are preparing to influence others by owning the air around you. Identity is the first step in telling your vivid life story because it positions you to grow, to contribute, and to fulfill the work you are called to do.

You get to decide if you will be the hero or the villain in your story. As the hero you will accept the responsibility to sink yourself into a careful exploration of who you are and the work you have been given. If you neglect that charge, sadly, you will become the villain agreeing with those negative voices.

Solving Your Identity Crisis

My entire career has been dedicated to helping people and businesses solve their identity crisis. The goal is simple: become everything you were designed to be so you can finish building what you were destined to create. One of the biggest challenges we all face is going through cycles of identity crisis. That is why I am here. If you are feeling uncertain about who you are or where you are headed, it may signal an identity crisis. Allow me to suggest three actions for breaking through: examination, exploration, and experimentation.

Let's start with **examination**. Any time you are about to embark on something important, you have to take inventory. One of the best ways to take an inventory of your identity is by using assessments. I have used many assessments over the years to understand different parts of my personality, and I suggest you do the same. One of my favorites is Gallup's StrengthsFinder 2.0. It helps you identify your core strengths and encourages you to focus on developing those strengths rather than worrying about your weaknesses. Another great tool is the BrainMap®, which helps you define your unique thinking profile. Our thinking is shaped by both nature and nurture, and the BrainMap® gives you insights into how you think and how to develop new patterns. I have more, but those two are a great place to start. (You can order them on my website.)

Next, let's talk about **exploration**. When we step outside of our usual patterns, we discover new aspects of ourselves. For me, it was the moment I began sharing my story publicly that I realized how much of my identity had been shaped by fear. Exploring new opportunities allowed me to redefine who I thought I was. Regardless of how you think instinctively, engaging in new activities forces you to think differently. One of the best ways to discover who you are is by trying new things. When you explore, experiment, and push yourself beyond your usual routines, you develop new patterns and learn more about what makes you tick. That is where exploration comes in—it helps you understand your identity through new experiences.

Lastly, since identity is not fixed, **experimentation** with new roles, challenges, and opportunities teaches us more about who we are—*and who we can become*. You cannot keep doing the same things and expect to uncover new aspects of yourself. Acting in a different way shifts your perspective

CHAPTER 3: Identity

and often helps you see that you are capable of so much more. Many times, our sense of self is tied to external things like a job, possessions, or roles in relationships.

I have spent decades helping others with their visions, but when it came to my own, fear and self-doubt showed up with a vengeance, like villains I had been carrying with me all along. Every mistake, every difficulty was another opportunity for them to taunt me, to tell me I was not enough. Each time I moved forward anyway, I reclaimed a bit of my own story. I was proving to myself that the hero in me was stronger than any villain. The effort paid off in unexpected ways. Someone said that watching me step out gave them the courage to try something new. That is what it is all about—courageously stepping out, growing, and establishing your identity in the process.

Take a deep dive into your personal qualities and experiences. What defines you? What drives your actions and choices? Do not be afraid to push your boundaries, try new things, and discover hidden talents or passions. Growth happens when you allow yourself to experiment with different roles, interests, or activities. Through trial and error, you will refine your sense of self.

In addition to examination, exploration, and experimentation, the cornerstone to establishing your identity is **evidence**. Look for clues and proof in your life that reveal who you are:

Personality Traits – What qualities stand out to you and others?

Gifts – What are your natural talents and abilities?

Feedback – What do people around you say, both positively and negatively?

The Work You're Drawn To – What kind of work excites and fulfills you?

What Bothers You – What injustices or problems stir up passion in you?

These are pieces of evidence that guide you toward understanding your unique identity.

Love & Self-Discovery

The Bible teaches us that the new commandment is to love God and love your neighbor as yourself.[10] How can you love yourself if you do not know who you are? Establishing your identity begins with loving God and knowing that you are fearfully and wonderfully made.[1] You were chosen before the foundations of the earth were laid.[11] Before you were even formed in your mother's womb,[12] your identity was known by God. It is your responsibility to examine, explore, and experiment to establish your identity. This lifetime is about growing into God's plan for you. **You will know you are growing when your *dream to have* transforms into a *vision to become*.** Embrace the journey of self-discovery, commit to learning who you are, and sink yourself into the unique work you have been called to do. Your neighbor will be grateful that you decided to love yourself.

Defining Your Identity

Defining your identity is a mix of introspection and understanding how external influences have shaped you. Here are some steps to help you explore and define your identity:

First, **take time for self-reflection**. Think about your values, beliefs, and passions. Reflect on the experiences that have significantly influenced you. What makes you feel most authentic and alive? These insights are foundational to understanding who you are.

Next, **explore your background**. Your cultural, ethnic, and familial roots play a significant role in shaping your world view, habits, and preferences. Understanding these influences helps you see how they contribute to your identity. Even if what you learn is difficult to face, it plays a vital role in helping you define all of who you are.

Then, **think about the roles you play in life**—whether as a parent, friend, professional, or volunteer. Each role reveals a different facet of who you are, and when combined, they create a fuller picture of your identity.

Do not forget to **assess your interests and talents**. What are you naturally good at? What activities bring you joy? Your skills and hobbies can be key components of your identity.

Consider your goals and aspirations. Where do you see yourself in the future? Your ambitions reflect what you value most and are essential to defining your identity.

Also, it is helpful to **seek feedback from people who know you well**. How others see you can provide insights into parts of your identity you may not fully recognize. Conversations with friends and family can be enlightening.

Next, **write it down**. Articulate your thoughts about who you are. Whether it is journaling, writing poetry, or expressing yourself through art, putting your self-conception into words or images will help you define your identity. I wrote a poem called *"Let Me Explain"* about this very topic, and though I wrote it, listening to it feels like a prophetic message given just to me. (You can stream it on your favorite music platforms. I'm Gwendolyn Faye there.)

Most importantly, **embrace change**. As you grow and encounter new experiences, your identity will shift. This evolution is natural and part of becoming the person you are meant to be. Through this process, you will come to see that your identity is not static. It is an ever-evolving set of characteristics that make you unique.

The foundation of your personal brand lies in knowing exactly who you are. This is not merely a process of listing qualities or achievements. It is an exploration of what makes you uniquely capable of fulfilling your purpose. Think of identity as the core from which all other elements—*your influence and impact*—stem. Without a clear understanding of who you are, the actions you take and the messages you share can feel hollow, even misguided. Identity is the anchor that grounds you, providing stability and confidence. It influences your beliefs, guides your decisions, and ultimately drives your life's work. Knowing who you are shapes how you see yourself, allowing you to stand confidently in your uniqueness without being swayed by external pressures or wasting energy with comparisons.

How important is origin to identity?

Your origin—*where you come from*—plays a significant role in shaping your identity. It is the starting point of your personal narrative, connecting you to your cultural heritage, traditions, and family history. These elements influence your values, behaviors, and world view. **Knowing your origin provides a sense of belonging and community.** It connects you to a larger group with shared experiences and history, which can be especially important in multicultural environments.

Understanding your origin also helps you appreciate diversity. It deepens your empathy for others by allowing you to see the richness of different perspectives. Furthermore, it can contribute to your psychological well-being by offering a stable sense of self and fostering resilience. When you know where you come from, you draw strength from the struggles and successes of those who came before you.

While origin is important, remember that identity is multifaceted and dynamic. As you grow, you may choose to embrace, question, or redefine certain aspects of your origin. Ultimately, your identity is a blend of inherited traits, personal experiences, and individual choices.

Earning a PhD in ME

Alert! When you are going on this journey, you are the most central and important part in the whole thing. When I was younger, I thought that the vision was the most important. The vision was everything. My way of thinking was, *"I'm going to prioritize this because it is impacting so many other people and doing so much good."*

Now, I realize that you are the beginning point. You are the foundation. You are the main ingredient of the vision as the keeper of it. You cannot do it by yourself, but it still begins with you.

I had the privilege of meeting a gentleman who I was told was the biggest angel investor in the state of Georgia. I was going through some old notes, and I had written down that when he evaluates an opportunity, he is *"betting on the jockey, not the horse."* This means that when he invests in a business, he is really investing in the entrepreneur—*their character, resilience, and ability to lead.* **I want you to take a moment to consider how important you are as a visionary and architect of your future.**

I have also heard that when venture capitalists are looking for a business to invest in, they are looking for the entrepreneur. Frankly, they want to see who you are. What is your character? What is your track record? The latter does not necessarily mean that they are looking for a string of successes. Track record could be classified as how you handle failure. How did you come back? What did you learn? At the end of the day, it comes down to who you are. You can

CHAPTER 3: **Identity**

have all kinds of ideas, but if you cannot write your vision, make it vivid to get buy-in from others, and execute your plan, your ideas will go nowhere.

At this writing, I am in my sixties, and I suppose like most of the AARP generation, I do not feel any different than when I was 25. I am still that hopeful, joyous, inspired soul who always wanted to be and live as an artist. You could say that I have been building my personal brand over a lifetime–*one heartbreak, one triumph, and one hairstyle at a time*. There have been turning points–*moments, decisions*–that led to shifts in my perceptions of myself. Most of the good thoughts came when I allowed my artistic self to step forward. One of the most notable was creating my jewellery line. (I know that is not how Americans spell it, but I use it because it looks like poetry to me.) It came at a time when I was *"rebranding"* and taking inventory of decades of marketing, entrepreneurial, design, development, coaching and management experience. I wanted to translate all of it to take me into the next chapter of my young life.

A passion for branding courses through my veins. After hearing my pitch for yet another business I had created, the Creative Director at my first advertising agency job once told me, *"I think you just like creating all these personas for yourself."* She was almost right. Actually, what I care most about is using everything at my disposal to help people live their lives at play–art, technology, music, words, miniatures…a crochet hook. Living that out has required that I allow the transformation process to have its way. I came up with seven signs that you might need to do the same.

7 Signs It's Time to Rebrand Yourself

1 You actually declare out loud, *"I don't care how I look"*… and it shows.

The truth is. You *do* care. We all do. You may have grown comfortable with your physical state (or just numb to it). Your self esteem may have taken several blows, but you care. It can be seen in the pep in the step of a makeover recipient. Don't you love those before and after segments when someone has been pampered and emerges looking and feeling like a new person? They are often overcome with emotion as they see how good they can look. Sometimes an external change in the form of a makeover can inspire vital internal work.

2 You feel sluggish and tired.

A lack of energy can have many causes, but one of the most common is a broken heart. When our deepest desires are denied or delayed, alliteration aside, we can feel defeated to the point where we do not have the strength to put one foot in front of the other. Another culprit could be your diet. As much as you love those processed foods, sugars, sodas, and your favorite dishes, our bodies were not built for them. Is it time to pay more attention to what you are putting in your mouth? Or do you need to mend your couch potato ways? It is simple. Basic nutrition, movement, and fulfillment create energy.

3 Your work does not give you joy.

We have all had to take jobs that we did not necessarily want, but staying in that situation can make you feel hopeless. I am surrounded by artists, musicians, and entrepreneurs. We all share a gene that allows us to quickly ditch the *"security"* of a 9-to-5 for the promise of wealth, independence, and real change. However, we often find ourselves so bound by our inability to pay the bills that we retreat to the *"safety"* of a check, only to repeat the cycle. If any of that speaks to you, or you just feel chained to a cubicle, know that the way out is through the process. Making your vision vivid is about working through the process over and over to make the adjustments that eventually bring you your life's work.

4 You cannot articulate what you want.

I founded Adam Red, a branding agency, to tell stories and create experiences. I kept running into people with ideas, but no understanding of how to bring them to pass. Since I can hear an idea and instinctively see the next step, it was a perfectly logical approach. I set out to coach the dreamer and provide specific services to manifest the dream. However, in 99% of the cases, my clients could not even tell me exactly what the dream was. Even if you are not trying to start a business or change the world, if you are going to get a better life for yourself and those you love, you have to be able to say what you want. Mind you, getting there may start with what you do not want, but the only way you will reach the positive side of that equation is taking the time to define what would be better.

5 Disappointment has overtaken you, leaving you afraid to try.

I believe we have regular dates with destiny—*appointments*—if you will. When we miss those appointments, when we are disconnected, that leads to disappointment. Langston Hughes asked, *"What happens to a dream deferred?"* Word Work is necessary here. A Hebrew Proverb says that hope deferred makes the heart sick. According to Dictionary.com, *"dis"* is a Latin prefix that means *apart, away, asunder*. It further explains that placing *"dis"* in front of a word changes its meaning in the negative. What happened? What have you been appointed to do and be? How have your *dis*-appointments affected you? I have been there. I have been so disappointed and frustrated that I could not love and live with confidence. As a result, I was unable to muster the strength to even try again. When did you stop believing in your childhood dreams? What taught you that it was unsafe to be yourself? Trauma leaves us afraid and stunts our growth–*physically and emotionally*.

6 You are not sure what you believe.

Did you start out in faith, but now you are questioning what you thought God said? Or even if there is a God at all? It is natural to question, to reevaluate, and test your assumptions. You were invested 1000% in that relationship, and you thought it was mutual. Now, you are unsure if you can trust anyone again. Did you follow all the steps and check off all the boxes, but it still did not work out? It is time to go back to where you started and take an assessment of the factors that were the basis for your original actions? You can use what you learn to discard what no longer works and fortify your foundation.

7 You resist change.

Change is hard for everyone. Our routines are comforting. They provide a sense of security, even if the habits are self-destructive. Australian world leader, Peter Daniels, famously said, *"Success is the willingness to bear pain."* I decided years ago when I heard this truth that I wanted to choose pain that produces, rather than pain that destroys. Change is happening to us every day, every moment as time passes. Sometimes it is out of our control and comes in the form of tragedy. At other times, it can be delivered to our doorstep by someone else. Quite often, it is our failure to act. Whatever the cause, learning to embrace change will lead to a vivid life.

Is it time?

Whether it is how you look, how you feel, or what you do, a vivid life is available. It will require that you simply verbalize what that is for you, face your fears to try again, pursue it from a position of faith, and embrace change. Expect it to hurt. They do not call them *growing pains* for nothing. Nonetheless, you will come through the process feeling stronger, more capable, and ready to face anything. Take inventory of the resources you have available to help you, and start there…maybe consider finding a Coach (not just one in your head, like now). Think about it, even Michael Jordan had a coach. No matter how capable, experienced, or talented, we all need the support, accountability, and encouragement to become the best version of ourselves. Your vivid life awaits, and it is worth every moment of struggle and uncertainty. Being self-explanatory is the payoff!

When something is described as *"self-explanatory,"* it means that it is clear and easy to understand without needing further explanation. It is the kind of information that most people can grasp immediately. Whether it is a concept, instruction, or process, being self-explanatory means that the essential information is obvious, simple, and does not require additional details. **Your vivid life story is about living life at PLAY with an established identity–*being self explanatory.***

Developing Your Identity Map

To navigate the gap between who you are now and who you want to become, you need a map—*an Identity Map*. This is the first of four maps that make up your personal brand maps to be included in your PLAYBook. It will help bring order to the complexity of who you are. **Your identity as a visionary is just as important as the vision itself.** Your identity is the foundation for everything. It determines how you approach life, how you make decisions, and how you pursue your vision. Think of your Identity Map as an examination of how you think, what you stand for, and how you show up in the world. The Identity Map includes several key dimensions:

Thinking Patterns: Your thoughts shape your reality. Identifying your thinking patterns helps you understand how you solve problems, how you process information, and how you react to challenges. Tools like the BrainMap® assessment reveal these patterns, providing insight into how you think and how others perceive you.

Behavioral Style: This is how you instinctively respond under pressure. It is your natural way of interacting with the world, and understanding this helps you navigate your relationships and environments more effectively.

Fears: Everyone has fears that hold them back. Personally, I am an optimist—*my blood type is even B positive*—so I naturally lean toward positivity. Like anyone, I have my own fears. Positive people often bury their fears beneath a layer of optimism, avoiding them in favor of keeping a rosy outlook. Yet, those fears can still hold you back, whether you acknowledge them or not. Naming your fears is a crucial step in addressing them. Recognizing your fears is crucial because they form your inner villain's origin story.

Motivations: On the other hand, motivations act as the driving force behind your heroic actions. They push you forward. Let's do some Word Work to dig in. The root word is *motive*—what moves you, what gets you up and going? It is important to define your internal drivers.

Strengths: What are your superpowers? What comes naturally to you? Focusing on your strengths, rather than fixating on your weaknesses, allows you to play to your natural abilities. Too often, we focus on what we are not good at, rather than building from a position of strength.

Values: What do you stand for? Your values are your moral compass, guiding you in all your decisions. Knowing your core values helps you live a life aligned with what truly matters to you. Once you have defined your core values, they become a guiding force, helping you make decisions based on what brings meaning to what you do.

Calling: Your calling is your life's mission, the reason you are here. When asked about their purpose, many people struggle to answer. Want to eliminate confusion and chaos? Focus on that thing that gnaws at you, the ache that will not leave you alone. That is your life's work yearning to be fulfilled.

Your Identity Map will help you walk into any room, secure in who you are, capable of staying strong no matter what comes. Leave the fear, comparison, and doubt behind. Heroes face them head-on and walk in their power anyway. This is not about perfection. It is about persistence, growth, and the courage to embrace who you were created to be. The hero of your vivid life story is you—strong, capable, and designed for greatness.

So, who do you think you are? Are you ready to become the hero of your story? Your identity shapes your influence, your impact, and your productivity.

Seize the Opportunity

Establishing your identity will require you to confront your deepest fears and challenge your preconceived limitations. You have the power to quiet the voices that attempt to pull you into either pride or comparison. They are the *"villains"* warring in your soul. You have the opportunity to become the hero capable of writing your own story. With each discovery about yourself, you reclaim the strength and resilience to make your life vivid.

Step forward with courage. Know that every facet of who you are, every challenge you face, and every step you take in faith is you seizing the opportunity. The hero of your vivid life story is not just someone to admire but someone to embody. You are that hero—*ready to glow up, show up, and grow up*. Do you see your cape blowing in the wind?

Every hero faces moments of doubt and seasons of struggle, but remember this. The hero's journey is defined by courage in the face of adversity, persistence when setbacks occur, and confidence in the possibility of a bright future. You are that hero. You can glow up with unapologetic acceptance of who you are. You can show up with unshakable confidence in what you have to offer. You can grow up with unstoppable determination to finish your life's work. The opportunity is yours.

CHAPTER 3: **Identity**

Re-VIEW [Identity Key Points Summary]

- Establishing your identity involves reconciling external influences with your divine design.

- Identity is not defined by societal labels or family expectations but by our divine origin–created in the image of God.

- Identity encompasses a wide range of factors—nationality, faith, personal experiences, and family heritage. Though we evolve over time, our spiritual identity remains constant.

- Comparison is the inner villain that tempts us to measure ourselves against others. This leads to self-importance or inadequacy, both symptoms of an identity crisis.

- The path to understanding who you are involves three essential actions: examination, exploration, and experimentation. Each one provides evidence.

- Key indicators of your identity include personality traits, natural gifts, feedback from others, passions, and the issues that stir you.

- Self-discovery is a spiritual responsibility because you cannot love yourself if you do not know yourself.

- You need to get so serious about who you are that you consider yourself earning a PhD in ME.

- Your Identity Map includes essential elements such as thinking patterns, behavioral style, fears, motivations, strengths, values, and calling. It serves as your foundation, guiding your influence, impact, and growth.

- Establishing identity involves seizing the opportunity to become the hero of your own vivid life story.

Make Your Life Vivid

Your A.C.T. List [Action to Complete This Task]

☐ **Define your values in three words.**

1 _____

2 _____

3 _____

☐ **Who are the villains trying to control your narrative?**

Think of the lies that have been spoken over you by yourself and others.

_____

_____

_____

_____

_____

☐ **How do you want to show up?**

Describe how you believe you are called to shine your light.

_____

_____

_____

_____

_____

CHAPTER 3: **Identity**

Resources

Identity Map Worksheet | 11" x 17"

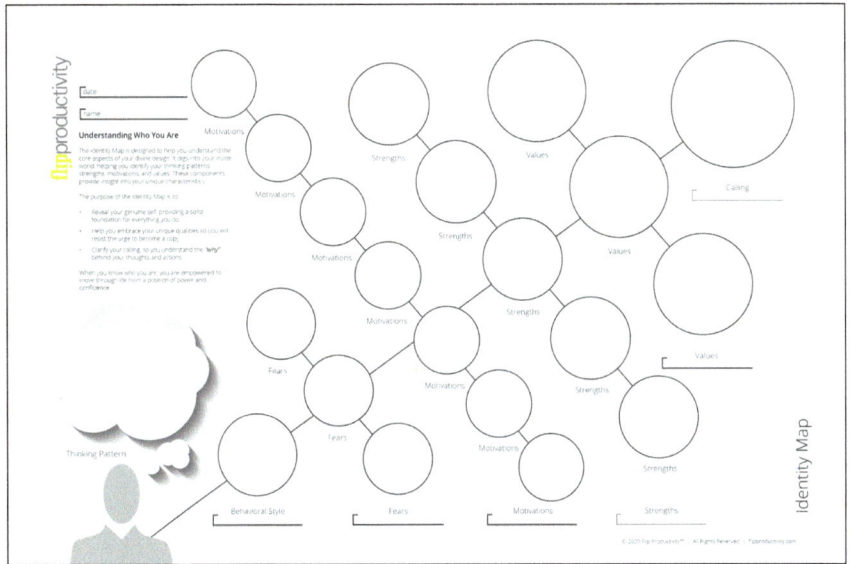

Recommended Reading

Discover Your God-Given Gifts by Don and Katie Fortune explores the three categories of gifts in the Bible with questions to help you determine your motivational gifts from Romans 12. This is a must-have for everyone interested in understanding themselves and improving their relationships at every level.

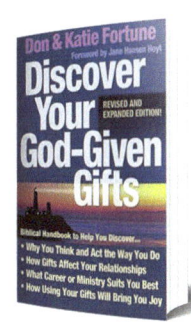

PLAYBook Toolkit

Visit playbook.gwenwitherspoon.com or scan the QR code to download worksheets, get video links, and other resources.

CHAPTER FOUR • INFLUENCE

You Are God's Gift to the World

[A RESPONSIBILITY TO BE THE ANSWER]

What problem were you born to solve?

In a world where influence often brings to mind social media stars, celebrities, or politicians, it is easy to forget that influence is woven into the very fabric of who we are. Each of us has a sphere of influence that extends through every interaction, decision, and action we take. Influence is not reserved for the famous. It is for the person who knows they were born to make a difference in the lives of others.

As a builder, your influence is not just about leaving a mark—it is about shaping the world around you in ways that only you can. You are not a passive participant in society. You have the ability to shape the culture around you. You were given gifts, not just to enrich your life. When we lean into discovering our gifts and using them, we do more than change ourselves—we uplift the people around us. Sometimes, though, we let the culture shape us instead.

It is easy to march in step with the values, beliefs, and behaviors dictated to us by the herd than to interpret them based on our identity and calling. To own your influence, you must first uncover the problem you were born to solve and recognize the power within you to be the answer. Reflect for a moment. What keeps you up at night? What are the issues or challenges that you feel singularly drawn to address? When you name these, you will begin to uncover the nature of your gift—*the talents, values, and convictions that make you irreplaceable.*

Influence Matters More Than Achievement

In a society that often celebrates achievement, it is easy to get caught up in the pursuit of external success. Yet, while achievements mark progress, influence makes an impression. Achievement is often recognized with accolades, while influence can quietly shape minds, inspire change, and reach beyond the immediate. Influence is the power to move others to action, to ignite their own visions, and to deepen their sense of purpose. It transforms mere accomplishments into something enduring, something that lives beyond the moment of achievement. It is one thing to celebrate another person's triumphs, but it is another for those triumphs to lead to greatness for others. That is influence.

Influence is also costly—it demands hard work, resilience, and a willingness to grow through adversity. Real influence is built on comebacks after setbacks, on the resolve to keep going when the mundane tests your endurance. Influence is built on the courage to overcome self-doubt and criticism. To wield influence, you must push beyond your comfort zone and be willing to strive for what is meaningful, even when the path is unclear.

Vision is what sustains us through these tests. Vision enables us to believe in what we cannot yet see, to persist when there is no immediate validation, and to continue when reward is not even a part of the equation. Vision is the lens that allows us to see through obstacles and challenges, revealing the bigger picture that our influence can help to create.

Discovering Your Influence In Five Builder Types

Influence is woven into your very being. It is the capacity to draw others in through your signature combination of strengths, experiences, and talents. To wield this influence effectively, it is essential to define the dimensions of your influence. These are the unique ways you can inspire, motivate, and impact others. On the way to creating your PLAYBook, the second personal brand map is your Influence Map. Developing yours will bring order to the complexity of the solutions your bring, how you are perceived by others, and the unique message you have to share.

I have identified five builder types. Each of them uses their influence in different ways. Keep in mind that profiles, categories, and types are useful to provide evidence of who we are, but they are not definitive declarations. You may resonate with several, but there is likely to be one that stands out for you. That particular type will point to your greatest dimension of influence.

The Thought Leader

Thought leaders bring unique perspectives and innovative ideas that inspire others to think beyond limitations. They offer transformative messages about purpose and growth and drive cultural shifts through bold concepts and a clear sense of mission.

Challenges and Blind Spots: Thought leaders can sometimes struggle with translating their big ideas into practical steps, focusing so much on the *"what"* that they overlook the *"how."* This can lead to frustration if others do not understand or embrace their vision. They may also have difficulty staying present as their ideas grow, sometimes isolating themselves from those who could provide crucial feedback. Additionally, the weight of high expectations can lead to burnout, especially if they lack a strong support system.

In Everyday Life: Thought leaders are not only found on large stages. They are present among us as teachers, community organizers, or even colleagues who share insightful perspectives. They are the people who inspire us to think in new ways, whether through conversations, projects, or simply by questioning the norm. Look for them in those who consistently bring fresh ideas to meetings or challenge you to envision a different future.

The Connector

Connectors build bridges and foster genuine relationships, excelling at making people feel valued and understood. They stand out by drawing people together with authenticity, vulnerability, and openness to connect deeply with others.

Challenges and Blind Spots: Connectors often find it hard to establish boundaries, as their desire to connect can lead to over committing themselves emotionally or spreading themselves too thin. They might also rely too heavily on external relationships for validation, sometimes losing sight of their own goals. This can lead to imbalance in their personal and professional lives if they neglect self-care in favor of always being available for others.

In Everyday Life: Connectors are the people around you who instinctively know how to bring others together. They are often the social glue of groups, from the colleague who organizes team-building activities to the friend who hosts gatherings to keep everyone engaged. These are the people who make it a point to understand and support you, often becoming the *"go-to"* person for encouragement or guidance.

The Performer

Performers captivate and engage others through their talents and creative expression. They influence by showcasing their gifts in ways that inspire, push boundaries, and create memorable experiences.

Challenges and Blind Spots: Performers face the pressure of maintaining public approval, which can lead to burnout or a sense of inauthenticity if they feel forced to *"perform"* constantly. They may also struggle with staying vulnerable, as the expectation to always *"be on"* can make it hard to show their true selves. Additionally, the drive for excellence can lead them to set unattainably high standards, risking their well-being for the sake of delivering a perfect performance.

In Everyday Life: Performers are not just on stage. They appear as people who bring energy, creativity, and a bit of flair to everyday situations. They may be the coworker who leads presentations with humor or the friend who turns any gathering into an event. Performers inspire us through their enthusiasm and passion, often motivating others simply by sharing their gifts and making life more entertaining.

The Storyteller

Storytellers shape culture and foster empathy through powerful narratives. They use storytelling to bridge divides, make complex ideas accessible, and encourage meaningful reflection.

Challenges and Blind Spots: Storytellers may become so invested in their work that they lose sight of their audience's needs or feedback. This can lead to creative blocks or frustration if their message is not well-received. They may also struggle with handling criticism, as their stories are often deeply personal. The pressure to consistently produce new content can drain their inspiration, especially if they feel compelled to conform to outside expectations.

In Everyday Life: Storytellers can be found in anyone who shares experiences that resonate to help others see the world in a new light. They might be a friend who narrates personal stories with humor and depth, a teacher who makes history relevant, or a family member who passes down traditions through insightful tales. Storytellers remind us of what we have in common, deepening our understanding and empathy.

The Advocate

Advocates are driven by compassion and a commitment to justice, often dedicating themselves to improving the lives of marginalized communities. Their advocacy shows up through their dedication to equality and amplifying the voices of the underrepresented.

Challenges and Blind Spots: Advocates are deeply invested in their causes, but this passion can sometimes lead to frustration when change is slow or resistance is high. They may struggle with feelings of isolation, especially if their views or actions alienate others. Advocates also face the risk of burnout, as their intense focus on a single cause can consume their energy and limit their perspective on alternative approaches to create change.

In Everyday Life: Advocates are everywhere—from the neighbor who fights for community improvements to the colleague who stands up for fairness in the workplace. They are the people who bring awareness to issues, pushing others to consider justice and equity in daily actions. Advocates remind us of the importance of standing up for what is right, whether in private conversations or larger social efforts.

These builder types represent not only famous figures but also the many ways influence takes shape in our daily lives. Each type contributes value while carrying with it specific challenges. Understanding them will enable you to recognize and cultivate your own influence.

I want to drive this point home further. Though we often associate influence with fame or public recognition, true influence is not always visible on a grand scale. Many impactful influencers live out their influence in quiet, yet powerful ways. A teacher who inspires her students to pursue their dreams, a neighbor who brings a community together, or a volunteer who dedicates time to mentoring youth—these individuals wield influence in deeply impactful ways. Remember, influence is not defined by a title or position. It is defined by your willingness to share yourself and your values in ways that enrich others' lives.

A personal example of this is what I discovered about my mother-in-law after becoming her 24-hour caregiver. In the months after my arrival, I learned so much about her extraordinary life. At 100-years-old, she had spent literally her entire life caring for others. She was not rich or famous. However, I was so struck by the consistency and scope of her influence, I could not imagine her life being summed up in just an obituary one day. So, I wrote a children's picture book called *"Miss Dorothy's Garden: 9 BEE Attitudes to Grow By."* I wanted to honor her work as a psychiatric emergency room nurse at San Francisco General Hospital for nearly four decades and at least capture a fraction of all that she invested in the lives of people. Hers is a legacy of kindness that I hope will live on in children and families for generations through the book.

Developing Your Influence Map

Now that you understand the diversity of influence, it is time to create your Influence Map. It is the second personal brand map for your PLAYBook. Consider what matters to you deeply and where you feel most compelled to act. Then, look at what **ideas** you want to contribute to the world, asking yourself, *"What progress do I hope to inspire?"*

Next, it is important to identify any **roadblocks** that may stand in your way. Just as a detour can cause delays, obstacles like financial limitations, knowledge gaps, or a lack of support can hinder your progress. By acknowledging these roadblocks, you empower yourself to find solutions, whether through partnerships, acquiring new skills, or leveraging resources creatively.

Equally crucial is understanding how you are **perceived by others**. What consistent feedback do you receive from friends, family, or colleagues? Often,

CHAPTER 4: **Influence**

feedback reveals blind spots and abilities that we may overlook. Embrace both positive and constructive feedback to get a sense of your influence.

Your **message** is also a fundamental part of your Influence Map. Think of the words that resonate most deeply with you, those that reflect the impact you wish to leave on others. Identify five emotions or outcomes that you want others to experience when they engage with your work or ideas. For example, you may want people to feel inspired, validated, or challenged by your message. A clear message serves as the heartbeat of your influence, helping you connect authentically with those you reach.

Lastly, define your natural **role in groups** or collaborative settings. Are you a facilitator, someone who helps a team operate smoothly? Or perhaps you are a creator, generating ideas and concepts? Maybe you are an advancer, taking those ideas and pushing them forward. Or are you a refiner, the one who hones and perfects ideas? Knowing your role helps you navigate connections, ensuring you bring your best to every interaction.

As you map out these dimensions—*your ideas, roadblocks, feedback, message, and role*—you create a comprehensive view of how you influence your immediate surroundings. Remember that influence is a long-game. Even when you encounter resistance, continue investing yourself. You may not see the impact of your influence, but you can be confident that it will be evident in the people around you in ways you least expect.

Facing and Overcoming Roadblocks

On this journey, roadblocks are inevitable, but each obstacle presents an opportunity for growth. Whether it is financial limitations, lack of knowledge, or time constraints, view each roadblock as a challenge to be addressed, not a reason to stop. For example, if money is a barrier, document your needs to get specific about what you require. If a lack of knowledge is holding you back, commit to continuous learning, identifying resources that can get you the information you need. In moments when support feels lacking, take small steps forward anyway, leveraging what you can control. The right people and resources often appear as you move with purpose. If time constraints are a consistent struggle, reassess your priorities, track your time, and eliminate what does not align with your vision. Recognize that every roadblock has a solution. It may require persistence and creativity to find it. As you overcome each obstacle, you not only strengthen your resolve, you show others that challenges are part of the journey.

The Call to Be Salt and Light

As you explore the depths of your influence, it is essential to remember that influence is about fulfilling a divine calling. In Matthew 5:13-16, Jesus describes His followers as the *"salt of the earth"* [13] and the *"light of the world."* [14] This declaration is not merely a poetic metaphor—it is a directive for living a life of influence rooted in love, integrity, and purpose.

Being *"salt"* implies that we are to preserve, enhance, and bring out the best in others. Just as salt prevents decay and enhances flavor, our influence is meant to uplift, inspire, and counter negativity. We are called to add value to our communities, workplaces, and families. Think about the preservative quality of salt. Your influence can increase strength, compassion, and kindness in society, preventing it from deteriorating into selfishness or despair. Influence is not about changing others to suit our desires. It is about promoting and providing what is good in the lives of those we touch.

In the same way, being *"light"* means that we are called to illuminate the way forward. Light offers guidance, reveals truth, and dispels darkness. When we live as lights, we bring clarity, honesty, and hope to situations where there might otherwise be confusion, deceit, or fear. True influence is not hidden or passive. It shines brightly, showing others a path forward. Our lives should point others toward truth, inspire hope, and encourage perseverance.

Through this lens, your influence takes on a sacred responsibility. To be salt and light means to go beyond the pursuit of achievement or recognition. It is about embracing the responsibility to be the answer. When salt and light are doing their jobs, they enhance. In the same way, effective influence moves subtly, purposefully, and consistently. What happens when there is too much salt? Instead of preserving or bringing flavor, it destroys and repulses. What happens when there is too much light? It hurts your eyes, causes headaches, and is blinding. It is possible to make a good thing evil by being so focused on bringing change that you do harm instead. It is also important to honor the sacred nature and responsibility of your influence by not abusing it.

Influence Requires Both Faith and Vision

Influence as salt and light also requires perseverance, dedication, and faith. When you embrace your role as an influencer, you are called to work hard, often without immediate results. Salt and light function without fanfare—*they do not need validation to be effective*. In the same way, the impact of our influence often is not immediately visible. Sometimes, it takes years before the seeds we plant in others' lives begin to grow. Yet, we are encouraged to keep believing in the impact of our presence, trusting that our influence is taking root even when we cannot see it.

This is where vision comes into play. Vision allows you to keep moving forward even when the path is difficult, trusting in the unseen results of your efforts. Vision keeps your eyes focused on the greater purpose, reminding you that each interaction, each kind word, each moment of courage matters in ways that you may never fully understand. Vision gives us the courage to influence with humility and perseverance, knowing that our role is to be faithful and consistent, leaving the ultimate outcome in God's hands.

The Breadth of Influence: More Than Fame

I want to reiterate that, while we often highlight well-known figures when discussing influence, fame is not the goal of influence. The people we recognize are known for the breadth and reach of their impact. That is what gives them notoriety. You may not see your name in headlines or have millions following your lead, but the value of your influence is not measured in numbers. Real influence lies in the depth of your relationships and the limitless boundaries of your reach. Each small act of kindness, each word of encouragement, and each moment of honesty matters. You might influence a close friend or a stranger, who then goes on to influence their family, community, or workplace, creating waves of positive change that extend beyond your immediate sphere.

The Price of Influence

Influence is costly. It requires effort, resilience, and a willingness to invest in the lives of others. Like salt that must be applied skillfully and light that has to be directed, influence demands intentionality. It takes working hard, triumphing over adversity, and continually persevering even when it seems like no one is watching. Yet, as salt and light, you are assured that your influence matters, even in the smallest gestures. Each act of kindness and each decision to live with purpose and integrity adds to a world that desperately needs the goodness you bring.

Influence is about more than the impression you leave. It is about the lasting connections you make. Influence involves choosing actions and words and making decisions that reflect not just what you do but who you are. Your influence gives you the ability to shift others' perceptions and perspectives. That is why developing your influence has to be intentional. The way you influence the world around you is an extension of your identity. It is how your values and beliefs reach beyond yourself. Through your influence, you share a part of yourself with the world, inspiring others and amplifying your message. Influence makes it possible to transcend the ordinary, and spread your uniqueness far beyond your immediate circle. That makes you God's gift to the world.

The Responsibility of Influence

To answer the question, *"What problem were you born to solve,"* you must explore the layers of influence in your life. The question goes beyond personal ambition—*it is a call to action*. Influence is not just a privilege. It is a responsibility to be the answer to someone else's need. When you think about the problems in the world, whether they exist in your community, workplace, or even in your family, remember that you were skillfully designed to meet this moment. Your experiences, gifts, and even struggles have been preparing you for such a time as this.[15]

Your influence is God's gift to the world. It is how He chooses to reach others through you. Just as salt brings out the flavor, and light drives out darkness, you are called to bring out the best in those around you. This is not about achieving perfection. Rather, it is about allowing your influence to reflect the grace, compassion, and strength that God has placed within you.

God does not give influence lightly. He knows the potential impact of each word, action, and decision. That is why it is essential to treat influence as a sacred trust. When you lean into the problem you were born to solve, you are

CHAPTER 4: Influence

not just fulfilling a personal calling—*you are stepping into a divine partnership.* God has equipped you with everything you need. Taking responsibility to be the answer makes you a conduit for His love toward humanity, shaping lives in ways you will never fully understand.

Embracing your influence means stepping beyond comfort zones, facing challenges, and embracing both triumph and adversity. It is about believing in a vision that is more than what you can see and trusting that each step forward brings you closer to fulfilling your God-given purpose. Influence, after all, is not about fame or recognition. It is about becoming the person you were created to be and using it all to make a difference.

Your Influence Matters

As you tell your vivid life story, remember that your influence is a part of God's design. Your life—*your words, your actions, your decisions, and your commitment to being the answer*—has the power to reflect His heart to those around you. So, ask yourself once more, *"What problem was I born to solve?"* As you live out that answer, know that whether or not the world knows your name, like my mother-in-law, your influence is felt because you have chosen to invest your talents, passions, and work as a gift to others. Each time you take a step toward the problem you were born to solve, you leave a mark that cannot be erased.

Consider the athletic coaches who nurture young minds, the mentors who guide others through challenges, the friend who listens without judgment, or the community leader who gives tirelessly. These people may not appear on magazine covers, but they change lives in profound ways. Their influence is built over time, through faithfulness, resilience, and love. It is the quiet dedication to serving others, day-after-day, that defines their legacies.

Remember, the reach of your influence extends far beyond what is visible. When you pour yourself into your gift, when you invest in others selflessly and work with purpose, you do more than create immediate impact—you build something that lasts. Your influence becomes a part of the lives you touch, inspiring others to believe and reach higher. So, as you consider your influence, know that it is enough to be faithful to the work at hand, to invest fully in your gift, and to give your best without needing to be seen. You just might become famous, but fame alone is fleeting. However, influence—*when it is fueled by purpose and rooted in love*—will be felt long after you are gone.

Influence carries with it a profound responsibility to be the answer. You cannot wait for *"someone"* to do something. You are that someone designed to lift and guide others. In a world where our minds are bombarded with competing visions, those who choose to intentionally cultivate influence are lights in the darkness, showing the way and adding value. Embracing your role as an influencer—*whether that influence touches one life or millions*—is an act of obedience to your heavenly calling. You have been given unique abilities to influence people. With those abilities comes a call to action. Will you accept the responsibility to use your influence to be the answer?

CHAPTER 4: **Influence**

Re-VIEW [Influence Key Points Summary]

- Influence is a personal gift given to each of us, empowering us to shape the world intentionally.
- Your influence is rooted in purpose. Investing in your primary gift allows you to address a unique need.
- The Five Builder Types:

  Thought Leader: Innovates and challenges norms, balancing vision with practical steps

  Connector: Brings people together, focusing on building community over broad reach

  Performer: Captivates audiences with talent, maintaining authenticity under the pressure that visibility brings

  Storyteller: Shapes culture through narratives that celebrate humanity and bring people together

  Advocate: Driven by justice, uplifting others while managing emotional investment

- Influence requires resilience and dedication. Roadblocks become opportunities for growth, strengthening your character.
- Embracing influence is a commitment to serving others, using your gifts to uplift.
- Influence is not about fame but purposeful action. Teachers, mentors, and community leaders show us how investing in relationships makes a lasting impact.
- Your influence is a sacred trust and God's gift to those around you.

Your A.C.T. List [Action to Complete This Task]

- [ ] **What builder types resonate with you?**
  Refer to pages 68-72.

  _____
  _____
  _____
  _____
  _____

- [ ] **What roadblocks are you facing?**

  _____
  _____
  _____
  _____
  _____

- [ ] **What problem were you born to solve?**

  _____
  _____
  _____
  _____
  _____

CHAPTER 4: **Influence**

Resources

Influence Map Worksheet | 11" x 17"

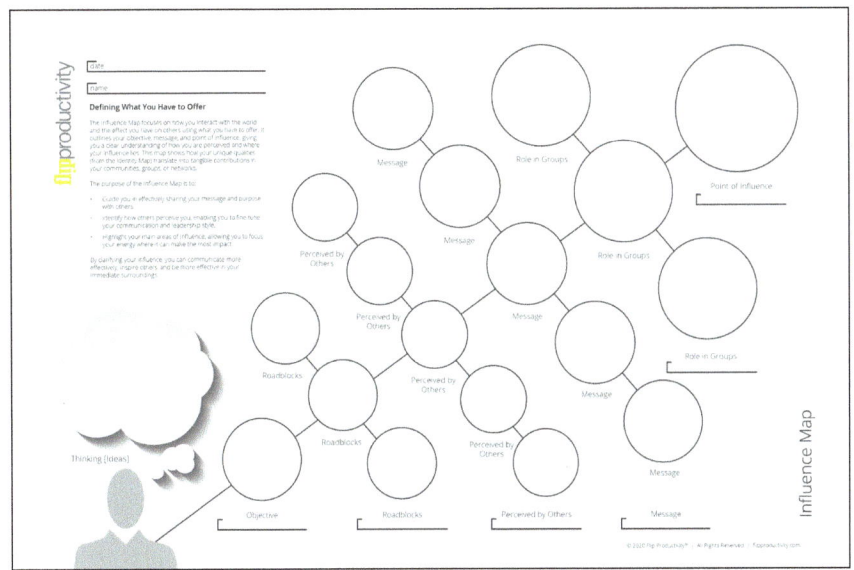

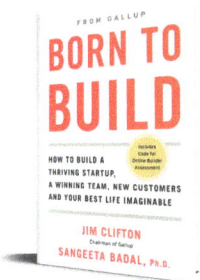

Recommended Reading

Born to Build offers a uniquely psychological approach to venture building. It gives readers the tools and techniques needed to understand who you are, what motivates you what you can build—and *how*. Follow the practical steps in Born to Build, and you will have the tools to build a sustainable and profitable venture of any size from scratch. *Includes Builder Profile Assessment Code*

PLAYBook Toolkit

Visit playbook.gwenwitherspoon.com or scan the QR code to download worksheets, get video links, and other resources.

CHAPTER FIVE • IMPACT

You Can Do Greater Works
[AN ASSIGNMENT TO CHANGE THE WORLD]

What are you called to build?

Have you ever looked at the problems faced by people in your own neighborhood, or all over the world, and felt powerless to do anything about it? Poverty, drought, war, homelessness, violence, illiteracy, trafficking, murder, hunger, sickness—*to name a few*—are pervasive problems. It is easy to turn away because it is so hard to see the suffering of others. The issues are so big, and the need is so great that it seems useless to try. We have our bills to pay and our families to care for afterall. With that said, all it takes is a change in perspective to realize you have more than you think—*more capacity, more options, and more wealth.*

    I left the United States for the first time ever this year. I went to Africa. It is hard to describe the experience, but I will try. To give you an idea of how I behaved, let's start with the flight. You should have seen me as I entered the cabin of the plane I would be in for the next fourteen hours. My instinctive response to the fabulosity of it all was to get everyone's attention, *"Look at this face,"* pointing psychotically to myself. *"This is the face of a woman on her first international flight!"* There was applause, cheers, and high fives all around as I practically skipped down the aisle. From that point on, I basically acted like a 5-year-old experiencing every day and every moment as a first.

    We landed in Johannesburg, South Africa. To say I was not ready is an understatement. I was not prepared when, as a passenger being driven from the airport to where we were staying, I screamed and braced myself for a collision because the driver was on the *"wrong"* side of the road. Yeah. That happened. The photo taken of me working by the light of my laptop when we were rudely introduced to load shedding later that night is still hilarious. I was so thrown off by the differences in currency, electrical outlets, measuring systems, paper sizes. It was a lot to take in. All of that aside, we were blessed with a tour from one of the locals who took us from the township of Soweto (home to landmarks of South Africa's fight for freedom from apartheid) to Sandton's commercial district known as *"Africa's richest square mile,"* and everything in between.

From there, we went to George, South Africa and stayed in a very wealthy golf estate. We returned to Johannesburg and drove to Gaborone, the capital of Botswana. We were treated to small, private and large, commercial farm experiences, and our favorite breakfast spot was sure to deliver a healthy dose of people watching, local flavor, and stimulating conversation with people who spoke up to six languages–*sometimes all at once*. We met a diamond mine owner, a fashion designer, a private school administrator, and *royalty*. Chicken and waffles were on the menu with a side of comfort, a dash of ease, and an extra helping of style.

My best memories are of the people. There were five of us on the team– *three Americans and two Africans*. We essentially lived together for three weeks as we traveled by plane and by car on a social impact mission. The teamwork around mealtimes, the laughs over cultural misunderstandings, and connections around faith, family, and purpose were priceless. Getting immersed in different cultures, being introduced to history in real-time, gaining a sense of the caste system and observing daily life was beyond interesting. I learned that the world is big and vast and that God is not an American.

In Africa, I discovered that we are rich. Our wealth is in our opportunities. No matter the size of your bank account, your ideas, intellect, and wisdom are the most valuable currency that you have. Before I went, a love affair with the continent had already been brewing. This thing had been going on for years via social media. My time there only sealed the deal. As friends of mine have visited and shared their experiences in other African nations, we have engaged in conversations about how we could make a difference for villages with no economic opportunities. We dared to dream of ending Period Poverty so that something as simple as access to feminine hygiene products would not shatter

CHAPTER 5: **Impact**

a girl's hope for an education. We even started a social impact marketing agency called Women of Rumble to launch a love invasion and end gender-based violence. We dared to set our sights on an Army of Goliaths to slay.

Last year, I built a social enterprise called Water Counts to solve our global drinking problem. I created a product that could be manufactured anywhere and sold to fund clean water projects. It is part of my 501(c)3 nonprofit, Vivid Academy, to support social impact entrepreneurs, create wealth, and transform communities. It was not lost on me that navigating the complexities of foreign governments, international laws, and culture would not be easy, to say the least. However, I was challenged to invest in and prepare for my assignment. If we are supposed to be salt and light, if we have been directed to ask for the nations,[16] and if we are here to do greater works[17] than Jesus himself, I need to be ready. The question for us all is, *"Will we dare to dream big enough?"*

Seeing the World & Your Role In It

If you will just open your eyes and change your perspective, you will begin to see the world not just as a place of needs but as a landscape of possibilities. This means recognizing that, despite the challenges in your own life or in the world at large, you are equipped with an extraordinary array of resources that transcend money or status. In fact, your capacity, options, and inner wealth are as vast as the vision you are willing to cultivate. You cannot be intimidated by the immensity of the darkness. My friend, Marje, wrote a song called *"Are You Afraid of the Dark?"*[20] The lyrics ask an important question:

Are you afraid of the dark?
Are you afraid of the dark?
Covered with light, seasoned with salt
Got that holy fire burning in your heart
Just so busy about ourselves, about our cares
My daddy, my mother, my sister, my brother
What about others who are lost in the dark, and they need the light?
They need your light. They need my light. They need his light, her light
Let your light shine that others may see your good works
Don't hide your light under your needs
Are you afraid of the dark?

Make Your Life Vivid

When our focus is only on our way of life and our personal issues, we cannot see that our capacity is greater than the demand we are putting on ourselves. While traveling in Africa, I was struck by the resilience and ingenuity of the people I met. From bustling markets to quiet villages, everyone seemed to embody a resourcefulness that transformed limitations into creative solutions. This resilience is not exclusive to any culture or country—it is a human capacity we all share. Within you lies an incredible ability to grow, adapt, and make a difference. Capacity is measured, not by the challenges you face, but by your willingness to meet them head-on. When you recognize your own potential, you realize that your contributions do not have to be grand gestures to make an impact. Start with something within reach. Our small, self-funded team started with literally what was in our hand.

When we see a need and simply begin to explore beyond our familiar surroundings, it expands our understanding of what is possible. Being in Africa exposed me to ways of thinking, problem-solving, and building communities that I had not encountered before. It taught me that there is rarely just one *"right"* way to create change. Your journey may be different from mine, but the principle holds—exploring diverse perspectives will uncover unique paths to impact. Consider the options that lie ahead of you. What innovations or solutions can you offer, and who can you partner with to amplify your impact?

True wealth is measured by your ideas, your intellect, and the relationships you build. It is easy to underestimate the value of these intangible assets, but they are among the most powerful tools for change you possess. You can create wealth by investing your talents in meaningful pursuits, by cultivating relationships that empower others, and by using your insights to solve problems. Take inventory of what you have in abundance—your skills, experiences, knowledge, and passion. Each one is a form of currency you can invest in building something that benefits both you and others.

I want to encourage you to see the world as a place where your unique gifts are necessary, and they are drawing you into a larger vision for your life. Just as my African experience challenged me to look beyond my own circumstances, I hope it inspires you to see your life as a powerful tool for impact. You can be an agent for global change right from your living room. You only need to recognize that you are equipped for greater works.

The World Is Your Playground

I mentioned that we stayed in a wealthy golf estate in George, South Africa. We needed a van to accommodate our luggage and get us to our destination. As we drove in, we marveled at the place we would call home for the next week. The driver starting telling us about the stunningly beautiful community. When describing the people who lived there, he said, *"They have too much money and no boss—like you."* Of course, we got a good laugh out of that, but it never left me. I am living life at play, and my vivid life has no boundaries. Since then, I have come to realize that I have the freedom to invest everything I have to offer to make a difference beyond my borders. How do you see yourself? What work have you been called to do? What do you want to build?

Let's do a quick review. We have been working on your PLAYBook, and it contains four maps: identity, influence, impact, and productivity. The first three are primary dimensions of your personality. They inform how you build. Though being productive is not a personality trait, you need a personal mission, vision, and values for disciplined action. So, whether you are focused on building your business, your family, or your ministry, your personal brand is the key to your impact and how you function in the earth.

On the outside chance that you still need to be convinced that you even need a PLAYBook or personal brand maps, I have three points that I want to make about the latter:

Your personal brand maps present all of the components of your personal brand in a simple and visual way. You will be infused with courage and the confidence that you are going in the right direction when faced with the unknown, even when the idea feels unsettling because you have not gone that way before.

Your personal brand maps will bring order to the complexity of who you are, who you are trying to reach, and what you want to accomplish. Order creates security. Seeing where things fit will make you feel like anything that you want to do is possible. You will be infused with strength, and that will make you feel powerful.

Your personal brand maps will reveal patterns and relationships. When you review what you have written on your maps at different stages in your life, you will see the relationships between all of these different complex elements. It is like putting a puzzle together and getting a clearer view as the picture takes shape.

Developing Your Impact Map

Like the others, we will begin this map with thinking, except here it relates to your world view. To plot your impact, you must first consider how you see the world. If you believe that the world revolves around your local community, your impact will be shaped by that belief. On the other hand, if you believe the world is vast and abundant, your impact will reflect that perspective. These are extremes, but they illustrate my point that what you believe about the world is the starting point for impact.

There has been a lot of talk in the last decade about finding your **tribe**. A tribe is defined as a *socially, ethnically, politically, or culturally cohesive group*. When I think of a tribe in the modern sense, I think of finding people who understand who you are and how you live. They speak the same *"language,"* think similarly, and may even look like you. That is your tribe.

What is your sphere of influence, your **territory**? Where are you meant to operate? This could be defined by your industry, life stage, or geographical location. In business, for example, you could focus on serving doctors or CPAs. You may address the needs of children or single mothers. You could limit your focus to rural or urban areas. The choice is yours.

Next, consider the **innovations and solutions** you have to offer. Even if others are doing what you want to do, they will not do it in the exact same way. What specific solutions can you bring to the challenges that your audience faces? What unique contributions can you make to the problems you are trying to solve?

What will be the impact of your **wealth**? When I speak of wealth, I am referring to abundance. True wealth includes being rich toward God, having

CHAPTER 5: Impact

thriving relationships, providing value through your personal brand, serving your community, being healthy, and having a prosperous soul. It is about living an abundant life that includes, but is not limited to, financial assets. I often ask my clients how much money they want to make, and it is rare that I receive a clear answer. When you create your Impact Map, it must include the wealth, in all its forms, that you want to create for yourself and for others and what you intend to do with it.

What impact do you want to have on your **community**? A community is a group of individuals who share a common understanding. They are interdependent and occupy the same region, interacting for social, professional, or educational purposes. Even if you do not know the people in your neighborhood personally, you share a common understanding through proximity.

Finally, what will be your **legacy**? What do you want to leave behind? I have heard of people writing their own obituary as an exercise in considering this question. How do you want your life to impact others? What do you want people to say about you when you are gone? Proverbs 13: 22 says, *"A good man leaves an inheritance to his children's children…"* My favorite definition of *"legacy"* is *maximum impact*. What do you want the maximum impact of your vivid life to be?

At the top of your Identity Map is your **calling**. At the top of your Influence Map is your point of influence. **At the top of your Impact Map is your legacy.** I do not expect you to answer every question I have posed right away. Instead, I encourage you to pull information from multiple sources. Write down some basic words and instructions to give yourself a starting point. Keep it simple—something you can easily grasp without much extra thought or effort. You can build on that later, writing more extensively about yourself. (Check out the prompts in the PLAYBook Toolkit on the resource page at the end of this chapter.)

Ultimately, each step in this process will help you gain the courage to take the next step and the step after that. You will find yourself at many crossroads in your lifetime, but you will have your PLAYBook as a reminder of who you are, confirmation of what you have to offer, and direction for your life's work. Your personal brand maps will encourage you, help you stay on course, and find alternate paths when you face roadblocks, giving you a chance to make your life vivid.

Who you are and how you influence people shapes your impact. When these forces are connected to your actions, nothing you imagine to do will be impossible.[18] This combination reveals that you were created to make a difference. Your impact, like your identity and influence, is a crucial part of your personal brand. Developing your **Impact Map** will reveal patterns in your relationships and the ways you contribute to the world around you.

You Are God's Greatest Work

You may have noticed a pattern. Each personality dimension map consists of seven components. In biblical symbology, the number seven represents spiritual perfection and God's work. That tells me that you and I are God's greatest work, and He has commissioned us to change the world.

Here is a summary of the seven components for each map:

Identity Map – thinking pattern, behavior style, fears, motivations, strengths, values, calling

Influence Map – ideas, objective, roadblocks, perception by others, message, role in groups, point of influence

Impact Map – world view, tribe, territory, innovation/solution, wealth, community, and legacy

You can download worksheets that I intentionally designed to be sparse, providing space for you to add color, pictures, and anything else you feel represents you. Together, the personal brand maps provide a way to see who you are at your core and the many dimensions of your design.

Your Personal Assignment to Impact the Nations

Your calling is not just about making a difference in your life but about transforming the lives of others. When Jesus said we would do *"greater works,"* He commissioned us to go beyond personal fulfillment and to become agents of change in a world that so desperately needs it. You can do greater works because you are equipped with unique gifts, life experiences, and a vision that is distinctively yours. This assignment to change the world is not limited to grand gestures or headlines. Sometimes, the most profound impact begins with small, intentional actions: showing up for those around you, offering kindness, or sharing wisdom that has been hard-won through your own trials. The legacy you build is the sum of those choices as you touch lives you may never even see.

The Importance of Impact Entrepreneurship

I said that we went to Africa for the purpose of social impact. Our team is building an international network of individuals focused on changing the world for good—*pun intended*. We want to end Period Poverty *for good*. We want to end gender-based violence *for good*. Our list is long because the world is filled with opportunities to bring change. While it is easy to feel small in the face of global challenges like these, we are not without power. This is where impact entrepreneurship comes in—a strategic approach to addressing social issues, whether you are a business owner, a community leader, or simply someone with a desire to contribute.

At its heart, **impact entrepreneurship is about creating ventures that aim to solve pressing social and environmental problems.** These enterprises, while they earn a profit, are driven by a mission to uplift, empower, and bring sustainable solutions. They answer the call to make the world a better place—*not just through charity, but through ingenuity and purpose-driven business.*

Impact entrepreneurship is not just for traditional entrepreneurs. It is a mindset that anyone can adopt. You may not see yourself as someone starting a business, but consider this—impact entrepreneurs are simply people who look at the needs around them and think, *"How can I use my skills, my resources, or my influence to make a difference?"* For some, it could mean creating a coffee shop and supporting growers in another country. For others, it might look like starting a local initiative that offers training and jobs to people in under-resourced communities. It can even mean bringing purpose to your current work or infusing social good into everyday decisions.

This approach requires us to rethink what it means to be *"wealthy."* True wealth is not just about personal gains—it is about using what you have to uplift others. It is about taking the wealth of ideas, knowledge, and skills you hold and applying them to real-world issues. Imagine leveraging your talents to create a product that benefits others, or using your network to open doors for people who are already doing it. This is the essence of impact entrepreneurship. It turns our ingenuity and sweat into a force for transformation, creating value not only for ourselves but for society.

Why choose impact entrepreneurship? Because it allows us to work with a *"triple bottom line"*—people, planet, and profit. Traditional businesses often focus solely on maximizing profit, but impact-driven ventures prioritize people and the planet as well, aiming for solutions that benefit all. It is not easy to balance these goals, but it offers a fulfillment that goes beyond financial success. Although it must be said that making money to make a difference is necessary. Profit is not a bad word. Having *"too much money"* means we can impact more people.

When we take on this mindset, we become part of a global movement to build a world where business and purpose align. Imagine what could happen if more people embraced the idea that work, when done with purpose, can heal communities. Impact entrepreneurship encourages us to be bold, to use our unique skills to foster positive change, and to inspire others to do the same. It calls us to challenge the status quo and use our divine nature to create real solutions. We have to operate from a world view that says there is more than enough for everyone.

Whether or not you consider yourself an entrepreneur, impact entrepreneurship is an invitation for each of us. It is a way to use whatever resources we have—*our time, talent, knowledge, or even just a compassionate heart*—to rise to this challenge and embody the potential for *"greater works."*

Wealth Creation As An Economic Engine

Wealth creation is a powerful tool for building stronger communities, especially in areas where economies are underdeveloped or non-existent. Impact Entrepreneurship does not just generate income. It stimulates local economies by creating jobs, building infrastructure, and providing resources that can transform entire communities. This approach recognizes that the cycle of wealth extends beyond personal gain. By investing your talents and resources into businesses that address unmet needs, you contribute to a broader economic ecosystem, one that grows and sustains itself over time.

When you commit to creating wealth through purposeful work, you are planting seeds that will yield not only financial returns but also social progress. By starting ventures in regions that lack economic momentum, you help lay the foundation for sustainable development. Small and medium-sized businesses, in particular, serve as critical economic engines in underserved areas, providing employment opportunities, fostering local talent, and circulating capital within the community. Each job created and each dollar reinvested strengthens the economic fabric, uplifting families, and breaking cycles of poverty.

Invest Your Life's Work to Do the Impossible

Solving the world's biggest problems may seem impossible, but here is the truth. These are precisely the challenges we are created to address. Each of us has a unique calling to make an impact, to build something that extends beyond ourselves, to bring light to darkness. This is the heart of doing greater works.

To answer this call is to see yourself as a builder—a creator who brings new possibilities into existence. What are you called to build? Your life's work is more than a job or a title. It is the vessel for your compassion, your courage, and your commitment to change. Whether you become a formal entrepreneur or simply bring a spirit of purpose and innovation to everything you do, you are empowered to make a difference.

Investing your life's work in solving complex issues is an act of courage and requires vision. It means recognizing that the *"impossible"* often just needs the right combination of creativity, resilience, and faith. Every action you take to serve a cause larger than yourself contributes to a future that is brighter, more just, and filled with hope.

Impact-driven work creates wealth on purpose. When you build wealth to uplift others, your success becomes a form of service. You have an assignment to live with purpose and direction, knowing that your life holds a unique meaning and calling beyond personal goals. It is about realizing that your talents, insights, and experiences are not random—*they are the tools and resources you have been given to fulfill a specific role in the world.* Being on assignment means accepting the responsibility to make a difference with what you have been entrusted, no matter the scale.

When you are on assignment, you approach each day with intention. You understand that challenges and obstacles are not detours but part of your growth, preparing you for the work you are meant to do. Being on assignment calls you to rise above comfort, to look outward, and to ask, *"How can I serve others? What impact can I make?"* It is about leveraging your skills and strengths to contribute something lasting—whether that is through small acts of kindness, building community, or creating systems of change.

This mindset does not just shape what you do, it shapes who you become. Being on assignment is a commitment to a life that transcends the everyday, a life that extends beyond your immediate circle to the world. It means being courageous in the face of uncertainty, persistent in the pursuit of solutions, and grounded in a sense of duty to live up to your potential. Will you embrace your assignment to change the world, to do greater works?

CHAPTER 5: **Impact**

Re-VIEW [Impact Key Points Summary]

- You have more capacity, options, and wealth than you realize.

- Embracing new experiences and cultures teaches resilience, resourcefulness, and a broader understanding of how to address challenges creatively.

- Rather than viewing the world as full of problems, see it as filled with possibilities.

- Creating your Impact Map—your world view, tribe, territory, solutions, wealth, community, and legacy—can clarify your direction and help you stay focused on the bigger picture of your assignment.

- Impact entrepreneurship is a powerful way to address social and environmental challenges.

- True wealth comes from investing your ideas, skills, and relationships in ways that uplift others and build stronger communities.

- Purposeful wealth creation can serve as an engine for economic growth, creating jobs, fostering community resilience, and breaking cycles of poverty.

- To be *"on assignment"* means living with intention, embracing your unique gifts, and committing to making a difference.

- The world's biggest challenges are often the ones we are created to address.

- Answering your assignment is a call to greater works—approaching each day with a sense of mission, creating solutions that matter, and empowering others to do the same.

Make Your Life Vivid

Your A.C.T. List [Action to Complete This Task]

☐ What are you called to build?

_____
_____
_____
_____
_____
_____

☐ What nation(s) are you drawn to?

_____
_____
_____
_____
_____

☐ What legacy do you want to leave?

_____
_____
_____
_____
_____
_____

CHAPTER 5: **Impact**

Resources

Impact Map Worksheet | 11" x 17"

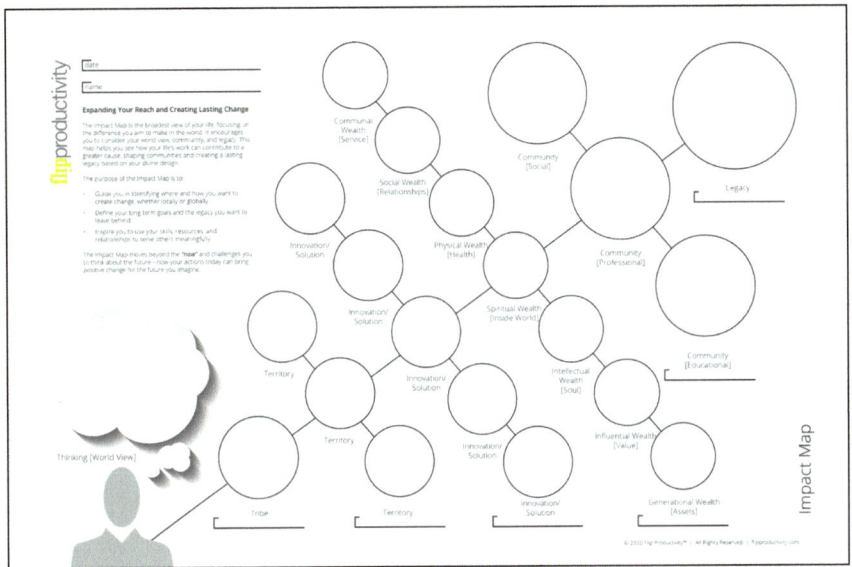

Recommended Reading

From a unique understanding of biblical principles, what Scott Nelson teaches in *The Economic Awakening* will help you position yourself strategically in this hour, gaining victory now and leaving a tremendous inheritance to your children and future generations.

PLAYBook Toolkit

Visit playbook.gwenwitherspoon.com or scan the QR code to download worksheets, get video links, and other resources.

97

CHAPTER SIX • PRODUCTIVITY

Six Brain Hacks to Command Your Day

[TOOLS TO TURN YOUR THOUGHTS INTO ACTION]

What habits will shape your future?

You might think that being productive is to get a lot done. I want to present to you a different way to define *"productivity."* It think of it as the act of turning your thoughts into action. How many times have you gotten an idea, but you did not act on it? Have you ever seen someone else implement one of your ideas, or something similar? If your answer is, *"Yes,"* then I am sure that feeling of loss is seared in your mind. You see, ideas are opportunities for anyone and everyone that will take action because productivity is part of your divine nature. You were born to produce. Let me tell you why I believe that.

I mentioned that I am the founder of a branding agency called Adam Red. My brother asked me why a woman would name her company after a man. The answer is simple. I did some Word Work about the name *"Adam."* It is derived from the Hebrew root *"adamah,"* meaning *"earth"* or *"ground."* Genesis 5: 2 says, *"Male and female created he them...and called their name Adam..."* So, Adam is not just the first man's first name, it is the name of *"mankind."* Stay with me. After he was formed, he was given work. His responsibility was to manage the garden. The first task in his creative role was to name everything God had created. (Adam was the first brand strategist.) This tells me that humans were designed to shape the world in divine partnership with God. Hence, **we were born to produce. We are makers.**

Let me share one more foundational principle about productivity. It is another that I learned from Myles Munroe. In his message, *"Kingdom Principles*

Make Your Life Vivid

to *Financial Problems,"* he explains that God withheld rain until He created a manager—*someone capable of organizing, cultivating, and stewarding resources.* This divine decision underscores a profound principle: **increase does not come without productivity**, the goal of management.

Productivity does not just happen. Productivity is the result of turning your thoughts into action. Productivity is a skill cultivated through disciplined management of your ideas, time, resources, and efforts. Your vision has to be managed. You must master your habits to manage your vision. Mastering your habits is the act of commanding each day, but the truth is, your brain will fight you every step of the way.

To master your habits, you have to first master your thinking. In this chapter, you will find mental models—what I call *"brain hacks"* to help you break through procrastination, find your words, and manage your vivid life more effectively.

Developing Your Productivity Map

Your Productivity Map includes your mission, vision, and values. They are not just for companies. You need them for your vivid life too.

Mission – What is your specific assignment? It should be a concise summary of the outcome you seek, who it impacts, the resources you will employ, and the territory you will affect. Your mission captures your purpose, guiding your daily actions.

Vision – What does the future look like? Define the experience you want to create for yourself and others, painting a vivid picture of the life you envision when your mission is complete. Your vision gives you a mental image of the future you are working toward.

Values – What principles guide your actions? Identify the standards that are most important to you. They will shape how you make decisions and provide guardrails for every action.

Defining your mission, vision, and values is an ongoing exercise, requiring reflection and refinement as you grow. Once you define your mission, vision, and values, you will have the foundation needed for effective planning and execution of your vision.

CHAPTER 6: **Productivity**

Brain Hacks to Make You More Productive

With your Productivity Map in place—*your mission, vision, and values as an anchor*—you are now ready to explore strategies that help you stay on course, accomplish your goals, and maximize your potential. The following pages contain an explanation of each Brain Hack designed to empower you with practical methods for clearing mental clutter, managing time effectively, and boosting your motivation.

Each one offers a unique approach to overcoming common productivity obstacles, such as distractions, procrastination, and overwhelm. Think of them as tools for rewiring your thinking and habits, so you can command your day. They will help you streamline your actions, reinforce your focus on meaningful goals, and ultimately make your life vivid.

My Brain Hacks are not quick fixes. They are techniques for developing a mindset that supports lasting productivity and fulfillment long-term. With each one, you will gain insights into both the inner and outer challenges of living life at play equipped with mental models to tackle them *head*-on. (See what I did there?)

Clarify Your **Vision**

Establish Your **Identity**

Find Your **Voice**

Uncover Missing **Information**

Commit to Your **Development**

Brain Hack #1:
How to Write Your Vision
[V.I.V.I.D.™ Model]

Writing your vision is more than just putting words on paper. It is about capturing the essence of what you are aiming for and making it clear enough to be understood at a glance so you and others can run with it. As Habakkuk 2: 2 instructs, *"Write the vision; make it plain on tablets, so he may run who reads it."* This process is what I call making your vision vivid—*how you describe and present the future you imagine*. A vivid vision speaks to all of the senses and inspires action—*from you and everyone who will be impacted*.

The **V.I.V.I.D.™ Model** stands for Vision, Identity, Voice, Information, and Development. This framework helps you get your vision out of your head and into action, not just through a single act of writing, but through continuous refinement. You have to write your vision on paper, on your mind, and on your heart to make it a part of you that you can share readily.

Let's dive into each element of the model and explore how you can make your vision come to life.

Clarify your Vision | *What's the big picture?*

Vision is about imagining a future that is better, brighter, and filled with possibility. It is not just a set of goals but a daring invitation to dream of a life that transforms you and those around you. Vision embodies your hopes and highest aspirations, allowing you to see beyond what is currently possible. It gives you a powerful sense of purpose, guiding each step toward a life marked by joy, change, and fulfillment.

This positive future fuels your resilience because it holds profound meaning. Your vision becomes a guiding star, helping you focus on what truly matters and keeping you grounded in purpose. Envisioning this transformative future inspires you to rise beyond the ordinary and live a life that uplifts others, making your journey as meaningful as the destination itself.

Establish your IDENTITY | *Who do you think you are?*

Identity is about understanding and embracing who you think you are and deciding how you want to show up in the world. Your identity defines you and shapes the unique way you approach your vision. It gives meaning to your actions, decisions, and interactions, empowering you to function with authenticity and conviction. Galatians 6: 4-5 tells us, *"Make a careful exploration of who you are and the work you've been given..."* You must know the core characteristics that make you who you are—*your strengths, values, personality, and experiences*. This self-knowledge helps you build confidence and resilience, shaping the way you pursue your goals and respond to challenges. Your identity reminds you of what you stand for and why your vision matters. It is essential to cultivate a strong sense of self because your identity motivates every decision you make and every step you take.

Find your VOICE | *What's your core message?*

Finding your voice is about discovering how best to express yourself. It involves understanding who you are, what you stand for, and how to communicate effectively. Your voice is how you express your vision to the world. It is about finding the right words, tone, and messaging that resonate with both you and your audience. The process of finding your voice is not about perfection. It is about starting to speak, write, and share your message. **If you want to find your voice, you have to use it.** Your core message will emerge after you begin. The act of speaking out—*despite insecurities or internal criticism*—helps you define what you have to say.

You must face the inner critic that tells you, *"You're too old," "You don't make sense,"* or *"No one is listening."* **If you do not write the book, publish the blog, sing the song, or make the video, no one will ever discover you or benefit from the solutions you were destined to provide.** The world will not change, and neither will you.

Your life is your message. As 2 Corinthians 3: 2-3 says, you are a living epistle—a letter to be shared with the world. We are waiting for your core message to inspire and inform us in a way only you can.

Uncover missing INFORMATION | *What do you need to know?*

Information is the missing knowledge or wisdom you need to fill in the gaps. No vision can come to life without understanding the landscape, the audience, and the challenges involved. It is essential to ask questions, do research, and gather the insights required to make informed decisions. Gathering information is the foundation for crafting a clear, actionable vision. Start by being curious. Ask *a lot* of questions. Be open-minded, ready to learn from everyone and everything. Then, filter the information you get by organizing it into categories to make it easier to review and apply. This process helps you build a library of insights that you can use to close the wisdom gap.

Commit to your DEVELOPMENT | *Who do you need to become?*

Becoming is not a project you complete—it is a lifelong process. You are not just working toward a vision, you are becoming the person God intended you to be. Becoming requires self-sacrifice, discipline, and training your inside world. **Like an athlete preparing for competition, you must be ready to sacrifice who you are now for who you are meant to become.** This journey will require controlling your appetites—*whether for food, money, or pleasure*—and redirecting your energy toward changing lives, starting with your own. Self-sacrifice helps you prove to yourself that you are capable of finishing the race, keeping promises to yourself, and becoming everything God intended. Development is the ongoing process of growth and refinement. Your vision requires continuous improvement—not just in your plans, but in your *self*. Growth is a lifelong process, and becoming your best self requires consistent, relentless, worthwhile development.

Using the V.I.V.I.D.™ Model will take you from just having ideas in your head to writing them in a way that inspires you and the people around you to run with it and bring it to pass. Put this process into practice, step-by-step. Then, repeat. As you clarify your vision, establish your identity, find your voice, uncover missing information, and commit to your development, you will see your vision come into focus. Your vivid life awaits, and the V.I.V.I.D.™ Model will help you get there.

CHAPTER 6: **Productivity**

Brain Hack #2:
How to Plan Anything
[Building the Ark]

In the context of vision, an *"ark"* is a vessel of hope, designed to carry you and your purpose through uncharted waters toward a new beginning. Just as Noah's Ark was built to provide refuge and protection in the midst of a storm, your vision is an ark that offers a way forward, a safe space to weather challenges, and a pathway to something transformative on the other side. Building your ark means creating a structure—*a plan*—that will carry you and the people destined to make the journey with you from where you are now to a future filled with promise.

The story of Noah is a profound reminder of the power of planning in the face of unseen challenges. Noah built the ark before the rains came, anticipating a need that no one else could see. In the same way, your vision is a solution crafted for future challenges or unfulfilled needs. Planning, then, is not just about preparation—it is about committing to your vision with the faith and determination to see it through, even when others may not understand its purpose. Your ark, your vision, is designed to provide refuge, stability, and a fresh start in the midst of uncertainty.

The *"Building the Ark"* framework offers a practical, step-by-step approach to translating your vision into a concrete plan. It is a brain hack for structuring anything from a business strategy to personal growth goals. The framework is built on five essential steps: Look Within, Look Up, Look Around, Look Ahead, and Look Back. They help you assess your motivations, align with your higher purpose, understand the environment, anticipate future needs, and reflect on your progress. By following these steps, you build a plan as intentional and resilient as Noah's Ark—one that can carry you safely through any storm to emerge with everything you need.

Turn the page to learn how to use Brain Hack #2 to plan anything, whether the task is daunting or mundane. It is the perfect foundation for any undertaking to solve any problem.

Make Your Life Vivid

LOOK WITHIN | What is this dream that you have?

Every vision begins as a seed planted within you, a unique dream that resonates deeply with your values, beliefs, and passions. Look Within is about uncovering this seed and clarifying the vision that is uniquely yours. This step requires introspection—exploring what truly matters to you and understanding the driving forces behind your desire to make a difference. By focusing on your internal motivations and values, you can create a vision that is both authentic and sustainable, rooted in who you are at your core.

- Ground your vision in genuine passion and personal values, making it more sustainable.

- Enhance self-awareness, helping you recognize what drives you and what fulfills you.

- Lay a solid foundation that aligns with your purpose, creating a vision that is uniquely yours.

- Strengthen motivation by identifying the core reasons you are committed to this dream.

- Help eliminate distractions by clarifying what truly matters to you, allowing you to focus on the essentials.

CHAPTER 6: **Productivity**

LOOK UP | Why is this worth doing?

Taking the time to understand the significance of your actions—*why they matter on a larger scale*—is essential for sustained growth and productivity. When you look up and connect your day-to-day efforts with a meaningful purpose, you can tap into a powerful source of motivation and direction that keeps you grounded and focused. This step is designed to help you discover the deeper *"why"* that fuels your journey, helping you see how each step you take contributes to a broader impact on your life, those around you, and even future generations.

- Guide your decisions with a clear sense of purpose for motivation and direction.
- Know why you are pursuing a vision to strengthen your resilience when faced with problems, setbacks, and failures.
- Inspire others around you with your dedication to amplify your impact beyond yourself.
- Act with purpose to build a lasting legacy that reflects your core values.
- Align your actions with deeper values to create a sense of fulfillment and integrity as you build.

LOOK AROUND | What's in your hand?

Once you have a vision and a purpose, Look Around to assess the resources at your disposal. Resources can include people, time, money, relationships, skills, and knowledge, all of which play a vital role in creating the future you imagine. This step encourages you to think creatively about maximizing what you already have and finding innovative ways to fill any gaps. By taking stock of available resources and identifying areas where you may need support, you can make strategic plans to leverage your strengths and increase your capacity.

- Encourages resourcefulness by identifying and maximizing what is already in your hand.

- Highlights potential gaps, prompting you to seek out or develop additional resources.

- Builds confidence by showing that you are equipped to take practical steps forward.

- Fosters creativity by inspiring innovative solutions using existing assets and relationships.

- Strengthens strategic planning by setting up resources to align with the goals and actions needed to build.

CHAPTER 6: **Productivity**

LOOK AHEAD | What's the V.I.V.I.D.™ View?

With a foundation and resources in place, Look Ahead is about using the V.I.V.I.D.™ Model to define concrete goals and create a roadmap toward achieving them, aligning each action with the larger vision. The V.I.V.I.D.™ View breaks down the journey into five actions: Clarify your Vision, Establish your Identity, Find your Voice, Uncover Missing Information, and Commit to your Development. By defining the big picture using the V.I.V.I.D.™ Model, you ensure that your vision is not just a distant goal, but a motivating force.

- Provides structure to your vision, breaking it into achievable and actionable steps.

- Maintains focus by creating specific milestones, helping you track progress and celebrate wins.

- Encourages adaptability, allowing for reassessment and refinement of goals as you progress.

- Boosts confidence and momentum with clear direction, so you always know your next step.

- Reinforces alignment between daily actions and long-term vision, ensuring consistency in your journey.

LOOK BACK | How far have you come?

Reflection is crucial for sustained growth, so when you Look Back you can evaluate progress and learn from each step you have taken. This stage encourages regular check-ins where you assess both your achievements and your challenges. Looking back provides insight into what has worked and what can be improved, while also offering a chance to celebrate progress and build resilience. By understanding how far you have come, you strengthen your motivation to keep moving forward, equipped with the lessons from the journey so far.

- Reinforces progress by acknowledging accomplishments, fueling motivation to continue.
- Promotes learning by identifying what has worked well and where adjustments may be needed.
- Increases resilience by highlighting growth and overcoming challenges.
- Inspires gratitude and satisfaction, helping you see value in each step, big or small.
- Strengthens commitment to the vision by reminding you of the positive impact of consistent effort.

CHAPTER 6: **Productivity**

Begin With the End in Mind

The key to planning is to know what you want. Following the five steps in Brain Hack #2 will help you create a simple, yet comprehensive, plan for anything you wish to build. This approach takes you from idea to action, with a structure that is easy to follow and share with others.

Building the Ark requires faith and foresight. Noah's task was not only to build a physical structure but also to create a refuge for life, anticipating a future need long before the storm arrived. Like Noah, you are called to build something that serves a greater purpose. Your vision, just like an ark, provides a safe harbor, a fresh start, and a solution for a future challenge, even if the need is not immediately visible to anyone else.

Planning before producing is essential. Often, we are so focused on getting things done that we forget why we started. Planning helps us stay grounded in our long-term vision, aligning our daily actions with our purpose. A vision alone is not enough—*you need a plan*. Building the Ark simplifies the planning process with five steps, covering every essential dimension so you can produce with confidence:

Look Within: Clarify the dream in your heart, the vision that drives you forward.

Look Up: Connect with a purpose greater than yourself to fuel your resilience and commitment.

Look Around: Identify the resources at your disposal, from skills to relationships.

Look Ahead: Define your V.I.V.I.D.™ View by detailing each part of your vision, using practical steps to bring it to life.

Look Back: Review your progress, learning from every step and celebrating how far you have come.

With these principles, you have a foundation for any plan. This process is adaptable, allowing you to revisit and refine your vision as you grow. Through this framework, you will create an actionable plan for something that not only addresses a present need but also prepares you for future success, making a meaningful impact on the world.

Make Your Life Vivid

CHAPTER 6: **Productivity**

Brain Hack #3:
How to Produce
[Clear the Brain Storm]

Producing is the process of completing a series of targeted actions. However, your brain is bombarded by a storm of thoughts that fight against your idea. Identifying the obstacles that cloud your vision is the first step to clearing what I call the brain storm. Quite simply, you need to get your head right.

Imagine your brain as a bucket with only so much space. When you get overwhelmed, it is because that bucket starts filling up with thoughts, ideas, and pressures coming at you from all directions. Eventually, it gets too full, and you just do not have room for it all. To achieve the goals you have set, you need to clear out that *"brain storm"* to be productive.

To get your head right, you must first understand how your brain works and recognize the mental roadblocks holding you back. When your *"bucket"* gets filled with too many thoughts, responsibilities, and pressures, you feel overwhelmed. You might juggle various roles—*caring for children, managing a relationship, dealing with aging parents, or keeping up with school, finances, and work*—all at once. To get anything done, you have to clear the clutter in your mind.

Think about it. We often say, *"I need to clear my mind,"* but what we really need to do is clear the brain storm. Your thinking is your biggest challenge. It can either propel you toward your vision or hold you back. It is not just the external pressures but also your internal dialogue—*the head trips you take*—that contribute to this clutter.

I have faced my own mental roadblocks. After over 40 episodes of hosting *Vivid Talk™ LIVE*, I found myself dreading it, feeling stuck in a brain fog. I even considered skipping an episode, thinking, *"No one will notice."* But once I started studying and preparing, everything clicked, and the fog began to lift. It made me realize just how important it is to get your thinking in order. Your thinking dictates your future, and that includes your ideas, beliefs, and emotions.

As an entrepreneur, I have been on a journey of self-awareness, learning to monitor my mental and emotional state. When things do not go as planned—whether it is about money, progress, or impact—I tend to slip into a negative mindset. I once noticed that I was perfectly fine creating with just five dollars, but if I hit zero, I would panic. You have your own triggers. It might be a certain bank balance or some other threshold that, once crossed, causes anxiety. The key is recognizing what those triggers are and how they affect you.

We allow mental blocks to form when we feel fear, frustration, or disappointment. These mental blocks can prevent us from making progress, so it is essential to identify what causes these feelings. Ask yourself, *"What makes me feel helpless?"* What depresses or upsets you? Once you understand your triggers, you can work on overcoming them and continue pursuing your vision.

Stepping into a vision I have held onto for decades has been transformative, but doing so required a new version of myself. My brain fought me every step of the way, trying to pull me back to old habits and ways of thinking. It was uncomfortable, yet exhilarating. This mental battle is something we all face when stepping into new territory.

The brain is wired to keep us safe, and anything new can be perceived as a threat. Your brain will resist change, even when that change is necessary for growth. This resistance is why you need to understand the difference between your brain and your mind. The brain controls bodily functions, interprets outside information, and protects your survival. Your mind, however, is the realm of your thoughts, feelings, attitudes, and beliefs. In biblical terms, it is your soul—*your mind, will, and emotions*. To manage your mental state, you need to know how these two interact.

Mental blocks and fog can show up in different ways. You might feel confused, unable to articulate your thoughts, or disorganized, especially when facing stress or when unwanted memories resurface. These blocks are defense mechanisms designed to protect you, but if left unchecked, they can sabotage you. Remember that inner villain? You need to clear the space in your head, challenge unproductive thoughts, and focus intentionally on what really matters.

To get your head right, you first need to be clear about your vision—*the big picture of what you want in life*. Then, you need to align your identity with that vision. Who do you need to become to reach your goals? Who are you intrinsically, and how does your design make your vision possible? This process requires a new way of seeing yourself and a commitment to shedding old behaviors.

Your voice is also important because it represents your influence. The way you speak reveals your true expectations. Align your words with your vision and your identity. Lastly, you must commit to learning new things and embrace discomfort. Growth always comes with discomfort, but it is the only way to develop into the person you need to be to achieve your vision.

Do not aim for perfection. Aim for progress. Celebrate each small win along the way. By focusing on these incremental improvements, you will develop the mental toughness necessary to keep going. You do not have to make all the changes at once. Start with one thing today and work on that.

Getting, and keeping, your head right is a constant battle, but with intentional focus, self-awareness, and a willingness to change, you will be able to clear the mental clutter and make your life vivid.

5 Habits to Master

Clearing the *"brain storm"* requires a disciplined approach to productivity. This brain hack is built on five core habits: organizing, tracking, acting, waiting, and scheduling. Mastering these habits will not only help you manage daily tasks but also give you clarity and focus, allowing you to move consistently toward your goals.

Organizing

Everything needs a designated place, whether physical or digital. Organizing is one of the best ways to clear your mind and create an environment conducive to productivity. Visual clutter translates into mental clutter, making it hard to stay focused or motivated. By bringing order to your surroundings, you are setting yourself up for clearer thinking and more effective action.

Benefits of Organizing:
- Clears physical and mental clutter, boosting focus
- Creates an environment that supports productivity
- Reduces stress by eliminating the chaos of misplaced items
- Saves time spent searching for essentials
- Reinforces a sense of control and readiness

Tracking

Tracking is vital to keep information, resources, and progress in check. Whether you are monitoring expenses, tracking progress on a project, or keeping a record of ideas, consistent tracking provides insight and control over your journey. If tracking is not your strength, delegate it or use tools to make it easier, but make sure you have a reliable system in place.

Benefits of Tracking:
- Keeps essential information readily available
- Helps monitor progress and make data-informed decisions
- Reduces overwhelm by breaking down complex tasks
- Provides insights that highlight where adjustments may be needed
- Builds accountability and transparency in reaching your goals

Acting

Lists are powerful tools, but they are only effective when translated into action. Moving from a *"to-do list"* to an *"A.C.T. List"* keeps you focused on completing tasks rather than just listing them. Write down your priorities so they are not lost in the shuffle of mental clutter. By taking action on the things that matter most, you conserve energy and keep momentum.

Benefits of Acting:
- Turns ideas and goals into tangible results
- Creates momentum through a focus on prioritized actions
- Frees up mental space by keeping important tasks written down
- Builds confidence as each completed action reinforces progress
- Enhances clarity on what needs to be done immediately vs. later

Waiting

Some parts of productivity require patience, especially when waiting on information or approval that is beyond your control. Write down what you are waiting for so it does not get lost in the shuffle. Waiting is not passive—*it is an active process of preparation and expectation.* Like prayer, waiting involves faith and readiness for what you hope to achieve, allowing you to stay focused while anticipating positive outcomes.

Benefits of Waiting:
- Reinforces patience and the importance of timing
- Keeps track of pending items to avoid missed opportunities
- Encourages faith and focus, even in periods of delay
- Teaches resilience and builds mental fortitude
- Prepares you to act immediately when circumstances align

Scheduling

A flexible schedule provides the structure needed to balance productivity and well-being. It is not about micromanaging every moment but ensuring your most important tasks have a designated time. Without a schedule, long-term goals like writing a book or launching a project can feel overwhelming. Scheduling allows you to create intentional space for what matters most and brings balance to daily life.

Benefits of Scheduling:
- Creates a reliable framework for time management
- Reduces procrastination by assigning times for key tasks
- Enhances focus by eliminating uncertainty about what to do next
- Balances structure with flexibility for adjustments
- Keeps long-term goals manageable and within reach

Together, these five habits—*organizing, tracking, acting, waiting, and scheduling*—are the backbone of productivity. When practiced consistently, they help you manage your workload, maintain mental clarity, and keep you moving steadily toward your vision. These habits are simple but transformative, laying a strong foundation for a productive, vivid life.

"When I _____ with **REPETITION**, _____ will become **EASY**.

When _____ becomes **EASY**, _____ will become a **PLEASURE**.

When _____ becomes a **PLEASURE**, I will _____ **OFTEN**.

When I _____ **OFTEN**, _____ will become a **HABIT**."

Brain Hack #4:
How to Change Any Habit
[REPOH]

Habits can be negative or positive, but they are formed the same way. REPOH is a mental model you can use to change any habit. It stands for: *Repetition, Easy, Pleasure, Often, Habit.* Use it to make any habit easier and more enjoyable over time, no matter the habit.

Unlike the other brain hacks, this one is not my own. I learned REPOH from Al and Hattie Hollingsworth at a workshop many years ago. It changed my life, and I teach this concept to others because it works. I always make sure to give them credit for teaching me this valuable lesson.

At the workshop, everyone in the room lined up single file ready to approach Al one-at-a-time to introduce themselves. He then asked, *"Can I be your coach?"* (I asked you the same question in the beginning.) We had to accept that invitation by responding, *"Yes, I will allow you to be my coach."* We shook hands to not only commit to him, but to *ourselves*.

I was a cheerleader in elementary and high school, so I really connected with it when we were taught REPOH as a cheer. We chanted and clapped to keep the rhythm, *"Repetition, Easy, Easy, Pleasure, Pleasure, Often, Often, Habit."* If you sing or chant something, it helps you commit it to memory faster. So, do it with me now: *"Repetition, Easy, Easy, Pleasure, Pleasure, Often, Often, Habit."*

To apply the REPOH brain hack, think of a habit you want to master. Let's use *"organizing"* for example. Here is how you would say it: *"When I organize with repetition, organizing will become easy. When organizing becomes easy, organizing will become a pleasure. When organizing becomes a pleasure, I will organize often. When I organize often, organizing will become a habit."*

You have to say it before you see yourself acting on what you say. The more you take action, you will receive the satisfaction of following through on the promise you made to yourself. Use the REPOH Brain Hack to change any habit for good.

WISDOM
OPERATIONS
O
REST
KNOWLEDGE
SKILLS

Brain Hack #5:
How to Become
[WORKS Model]

The vivid life is a life at play–*effectively doing, while delightfully being*. Doing is about work. Delightfully being while you work is made possible with Wisdom, Operations, Rest, Knowledge, and Skills. The W.O.R.K.S. Model will help you align your actions to become who God destined you to be.

WISDOM: The Foundation for Sound Decisions

In today's world, there is no shortage of information. You can find training online for just about anything, but information alone does not equate to wisdom. Wisdom is the ability to apply what you know to your specific situation, considering all the related factors. It is the insight to know the right course of action. As you gain experience—*and fail along the way*—you can employ wisdom to make sound decisions, navigate challenges, and apply the lessons learned.

- Helps you distinguish between information and insight, guiding choices with discernment
- Builds resilience by applying learned experiences to new challenges
- Encourages a proactive approach to seek mentorship and coaching
- Fills the *"wisdom gap"* by turning failures and setbacks into learning opportunities
- Aligns actions with long-term vision, fostering steady, purpose-driven growth

OPERATIONS: Making Vision Work

Operations are the systems and processes that make your ideas and your team work. Your vision is the story you tell, but your operations are the strategy that makes that vision a reality. Effective operations create an experience that includes your audience in your story, transforming casual interactions into lasting relationships.

Operations allow you to:
- Seamlessly integrate strategy, technology, and creativity
- Manage complexity through automation
- Establish a presence that captivates and retains your audience
- Execute your vision consistently and effectively
- Streamline communication and collaboration, ensuring that your team is aligned and focused on shared goals

REST: A Celebration of Work

Rest is not just about taking a break. It is about celebrating your work and progress. Rest replenishes your energy, increases focus, and promotes overall well-being. It is a time to clear your mind, reflect on your progress, and prepare for the next steps.

Rest is essential for sustainable productivity. Find activities that replenish you instead of deplete you. When rest is built into your schedule, it becomes part of a balanced lifestyle that promotes long-term health and well-being.

- Provides a mental and physical reset, ensuring long-term sustainability
- Reinforces a balanced lifestyle, integrating breaks into your workflow
- Invites reflection, allowing you to evaluate your progress and adjust your approach
- Helps prevent burnout, sustaining your motivation and enthusiasm
- Acts as a reward, celebrating milestones and achievements

KNOWLEDGE: Fuel for Growth

Knowledge is the fuel for growth. It is gathered through research, study, and observation, but it is only through applying that knowledge that true learning happens. Every bit of information you acquire is a stepping stone toward the wisdom that will guide your decisions.

You may know something, but understanding how to apply that knowledge to your assignment is critical. It is not enough to gather information—*you must*

know how to use it to fulfill your vision.
- Encourages lifelong learning, fueling your continuous development
- Cultivates curiosity, inspiring you to seek new insights and skills
- Serves as a foundation for wisdom, empowering informed, strategic decisions
- Helps clarify complex issues, enabling you to find effective solutions
- Bridges gaps in understanding, enhancing your ability to execute vision effectively

SKILLS: The Practical Application of Knowledge

Skills represent the competence and ability developed through practice, training, and repetition. It requires discipline to become proficient, and you will not gain skills overnight. Skills are honed through hard work and dedication.

Galatians 6: 4-5 The Message gives us a mandate: *"Make a careful exploration of who you are and the work you've been given, and then sink yourself into that. Don't be impressed with yourself. Don't compare yourself with others. Each of you must take responsibility for doing the creative best you can with your own life."*

Skills are the tangible result of consistent effort. Mastering a skill takes time, but the more you practice, the more you can contribute meaningfully.
- Transforms knowledge into practical ability, enhancing competency
- Builds confidence through repetition and mastery
- Enables creative problem-solving, allowing you to adapt to new challenges
- Adds value to your work, improving quality and impact
- Fosters self-reliance, empowering you to tackle tasks independently and effectively

Becoming is not passive—*it is an active process of growth*. The W.O.R.K.S. Model is designed to help you embrace that process, bridging the wisdom gap between where you are now and where you want to be. Each element—*Wisdom, Operations, Rest, Knowledge, and Skills*—builds on the others to create a holistic approach to personal and professional development.

PURPOSED

LIBERATED

ALIGNED

YIELDED

Brain Hack #6:
How to Live Life At Play
[PLAY Formula & Model]

In your journey toward a vivid life, understanding how to live life at play is crucial. This concept goes beyond simple entertainment or leisure. It is about integrating joy, purpose, and rest into every facet of your existence, transforming the mundane into a meaningful experience. Imagine a lifestyle where stress does not consume you, where learning and innovation flourish, and where relationships deepen. Living life at play is defined as *effectively doing, while delightfully being*. It is creating a harmonious blend of work that fulfills as you become the best version of yourself.

The Play Formula

The Play Formula emphasizes using your inherent strengths, finding meaning, and spending your time doing work based on those factors.

Strengths + Meaning / Time = Play

This formula encourages you to focus on activities that naturally align with your talents and values, creating a lifestyle where work is bringing out the best in you. When you connect your strengths (what you excel at naturally) with meaning (what matters most to you) and invest your time purposefully, you are living life at play.

The Play Formula teaches you to:

- Recognize and build on your strengths to make your weaknesses irrelevant
- Embed meaning into your work to align it with your deepest values
- Invest your time currency in meaningful activities for increased satisfaction
- Create a sense of flow where work does not drain you but energizes you
- Develop habits that make productivity feel effortless and joyful

The PLAY Model

While the Play Formula focuses on using your strengths, finding meaning, and spending your time based on those two factors, the PLAY Model serves as a framework for effectiveness and delight. PLAY is an acronym for Purposed, Liberated, Aligned, and Yielded.

PURPOSED – **Getting up each day with intention, driven by a clear sense of your God-given mission**

- Embrace daily action toward your destiny with confidence.
- Anchor your decisions in your values and goals.
- Cultivate resilience by staying focused on long-term aspirations.
- Recognize each step as a part of your larger purpose.
- Build routines that support intentional living.

LIBERATED – **Living free of limiting beliefs and constraints that hinder growth**

- Embrace authenticity in your relationships and pursuits.
- Discard fears that hold you back from reaching your potential.
- Recognize freedom as a pathway to live fully.
- Identify and release habits that no longer serve your purpose.
- Commit to nurturing a life where you feel free to explore and create.

ALIGNED – **Ensuring that your actions are in harmony with your unique rhythm and vision**

- Align your decisions with your personal and spiritual values.

CHAPTER 6: **Productivity**

- Focus on tasks that support your highest priorities.
- Minimize distractions by staying centered on your goals.
- Foster an inner peace that enhances productivity.
- Cultivate routines that support a balanced, focused lifestyle.

Yielded – Surrendering the struggle and trusting the process of growth

- Accept life's uncertainties as part of the journey.
- Trust in timing, knowing you are exactly where you need to be.
- Practice patience, even during challenging moments.
- Embrace humility, allowing yourself to learn and grow.
- Surrender control and open yourself to new possibilities.

This is what *effectively doing, while delightfully being* looks like. Living life at play means embracing challenges with resilience, fostering joy in daily tasks, and aligning your actions with your true purpose. Integrating the Play Formula and PLAY Model into your life creates a lifestyle that blends your life's work with who you are seamlessly, creating a framework for you to thrive. This is how you create a vivid life—by transforming every day into an opportunity to engage in what you do best and love most.

Re-VIEW [Productivity Key Points Summary]

- Think of productivity as turning thoughts into action, not just completing tasks.
- You were born to produce, reflecting your purpose to shape the world in partnership with God.
- Productivity is the key to increase. God does not bless based on what you pray for. He increases what you can manage.
- Productivity is developed through disciplined management of ideas, time, resources, and action.
- To effectively manage your vision, you need to master your habits and your thoughts.
- Productivity Map Components:

  Mission: Define your specific assignment, outcome, impact, resources, and territory.

  Vision: Envision the future you want to create and the experience you desire for yourself and others.

  Values: Identify your guiding principles to shape decisions and stay true to yourself.
- Use mental models as brain hacks to overcome procrastination, distractions, and overwhelm.
- Brain Hacks are tools to support a vivid life by building a productive mindset that endures over time.

Resources

Brain Hack #1: How to Write Your Vision [V.I.V.I.D.™ Model]
Vivid Session Questions Google Doc

Brain Hack #2: How to Plan Anything [Building the Ark]
Flip Productivity™ Plan Worksheet Fillable PDF

Brain Hack #3: How to Produce [Clear the Brain Storm]
- Flip Productivity™ Brain Storm Worksheet
- Flip Productivity™ Produce Worksheet | Actions Fillable PDF

Brain Hack #4: How to Change Any Habit [REPOH]
Flip Productivity™ Produce Worksheet | Habits Fillable PDF

Brain Hack #6: How to Live Life At Play [PLAY Formula & Model]
Flip Productivity™ Play Worksheet Fillable PDF

PLAYBook Toolkit

Visit playbook.gwenwitherspoon.com or scan the QR code to download worksheets, get video links, and other resources.

CHAPTER SEVEN • LIVING LIFE AT PLAY

Live Purposed, Liberated, Aligned, & Yielded

[A DARE TO RECAPTURE YOUR CHILDLIKE WONDER]

What is your unique PLAYBook?

Chapter One is about resisting the urge to be a copy of someone else, but how do you do that with all of the pressure to conform? From a young age, we are taught to seek approval, to blend in, and to follow paths laid out for us by others. Society, friends, and even family can unintentionally impose their ideas of who we should be. Without realizing it, we begin to gradually shrink. All too often, in an effort to be humble, we end up just dimming the light we were born with. Who told you it was not okay to be you? When did you discover it was not safe to speak your mind, share your ideas, or stand out?

This chapter invites you to rediscover your childlike wonder—reclaiming the satisfaction of dreaming, exploring, and creating without limits. Psychologists tell us that the age of five is a crucial time in a child's development, a period when they form their sense of self, independence, and curiosity. At this age, children live fully in the moment, eager to try new things, make friends, and express their uniqueness with a freedom we often lose as adults. Children approach life with openness, ready to explore without fear of failure or self-judgment. They see the world as a playground and each day as an opportunity to learn and laugh.

Children are natural visionaries. Their world is boundless, alive with imagination and endless possibilities. They can transform a simple stick into a magic wand, turn a cardboard box into a spaceship, and see heroes and giants in the ordinary. This capacity to dream without limits is one of the most precious qualities of childhood—an openness to the unknown, unburdened by self-doubt or the need to *"get it right."* Jesus understood the power of a child's heart, and that is why He said in Matthew 19: 14, *"Let the little children come to me, and do not hinder them, for the kingdom of heaven belongs to such as these."* He calls us to approach life and faith with that same openness, trust, and imagination—to bring our whole selves, unguarded and willing to see the miraculous all around us. When we come to Him with a childlike spirit, we unlock a realm of possibilities that only a trusting heart can access.

You are invited to return to that place of wonder and imagination. What if you allowed yourself to dream boldly again, to reimagine your world, not as it is, but as it could be? We all start out this way, but as time passes, we give into internal and external restrictions placed on us. As adults, we often trade our imagination for *"reality."* Responsibilities, expectations, disappointments, and even trauma can make us cautious instead of curious. As your coach, I want to invite you to break free. How would you feel if you could reclaim your childlike wonder and open new doors in your mind and heart? What would happen if you let go of the pressures to conform and gave yourself permission to approach life like a child at play? What would you dare to do? Who would you become? What is the world missing out on from you?

You Need a Personal Brand Guide

Creating your PLAYBook is an opportunity to craft a personal brand guide—*a blend of vision board, scrapbook, and journal*—that captures your dreams, goals, and triumphs. Let it be a place where you can freely capture your ideas, aspirations, and milestones as you rediscover what lights you up. Imagine each page as a playground for your thoughts and a blueprint for a vivid life at play: *purposed, liberated, aligned, and yielded.*

This PLAYBook is where your vivid life story will take shape, page-by-page, as you rediscover the beauty of living authentically and the thrill of following your unique path. Reclaim your childlike wonder, and let it fuel a life that feels both productive and playful. Your PLAYBook is not just a collection of goals or plans. It is an evolving document that reflects your dreams, values, and growth. Your PLAYBook is your personal brand guide as your vivid life unfolds.

Living life at play is the new self care. It means approaching each day with openness, allowing your work, relationships, and aspirations to feel like a natural, awe-inspiring extension of who you were created to be.

You Are a Work of Art

Have you ever considered yourself a masterpiece? Ephesians 2: 10, says, *"We are God's handiwork, created in Christ Jesus to do good works, which God prepared in advance for us to do."* This powerful statement invites us to see ourselves as intentional creations, crafted by the ultimate artist with precision and purpose. Like any masterpiece, we were formed thoughtfully, with beauty woven into every detail of who we are. You are not an accident or an afterthought. You are the expression of God's creativity, carefully designed to reflect His vision for your identity, influence, and impact.

A true work of art is not mass-produced. Each brushstroke, every chisel mark, is placed intentionally to serve a purpose and tell a story. So it is with you. Every experience, skill, and characteristic that makes you *"you"* is part of God's intricate design. When He formed you, He knew the gifts you would need, the resilience you would develop, and the challenges you would overcome. Just as an artist considers the purpose of a sculpture or the meaning behind a painting, God has designed you to fulfill a distinct role—*to express His love in the world.*

Accepting that you are God's handiwork also means embracing your individuality. In a world that often pressures us to conform, to fit into molds, God calls you to stand out as His unique creation. He did not create you to blend in. He designed you to be a expression of His image, with distinct qualities. Your voice, talents, and perspective are like vibrant colors on the canvas of His creation, and He invites you to use them fully and boldly.

Like any masterpiece, you are in progress. You will not see the full picture or understand every detail of how your story will unfold. Nevertheless, you can trust that God, the Master Artist, sees the end from the beginning. Each season, all of the laughter, and even the hardship, is part of His brushwork, layering depth and beauty into your vivid life story. He is still shaping you, refining you to reflect His glory more clearly. So, embrace the journey with confidence. You are God's work of art, set apart for a purpose that only you can fulfill.

Just as a brand carries distinct attributes that define its identity and purpose, so do you. See yourself as a personal brand crafted by God, each characteristic—*your strengths, quirks, passions, and even your struggles*—is part of the work He is doing in you. Like any effective brand, your attributes set you apart—the values you hold dear, the talents that come naturally, and the effect you have on those around you. These attributes are not random. They are intentionally woven into who you are to play a specific role in the world. Just as successful brands stay true to their core values, you are called to live authentically, rooted in the identity God has given you. When you align your actions and decisions with this divine brand identity, you reflect the fullness of who you were made to be, creating a powerful and consistent story that will resonate with others as you fulfill your God-given purpose.

The Science of Your Creation: Wonderful & Complex

You are not here by accident. Your very being is a masterpiece of divine engineering, with layers of complexity designed to work in perfect harmony. Modern science reveals that each of us is a tapestry of intricate biological systems, shaped by DNA, neurological wiring, and an ecosystem of cells that communicate, adapt, and grow in response to our environment. From the exact shade of your eyes to the unique patterns of your fingerprints, every detail is coded in your DNA—*an instruction manual that has no replica in the world*. With over 30 trillion cells that constantly work to keep you alive and thriving, your body is a marvel of creation that scientists continue to explore and are amazed by.

The brain alone, often called the most complex structure in the known universe, holds more than 86 billion neurons that form connections to shape your thoughts, memories, and personality. These neurons do not just act individually. They work in networks, adapting and reorganizing throughout your life, a phenomenon known as neuroplasticity. This capacity allows you to learn, heal, and grow, giving you the power to change and adapt in ways that bring renewal and transformation.

Psalm 139: 14 beautifully captures the miracle of your design, saying, *"I praise you because I am fearfully and wonderfully made; your works are wonderful,*

I know that full well." Science may tell us how we are made, but this scripture tells us why. We are works of God's craftsmanship, made intentionally and wonderfully for a purpose. When you consider both the science and the divine intention behind your existence, it becomes clear that you are crafted with immense care, precision, and love, meant to play a unique role that no one else can.

Understanding Your Psychology

I told you I want to get in your head. Your excuses, brain fog, mental blocks, torment, and emotional gymnastics are not accidental either. Your thinking is the key to your future. It is connected to everything—*your ideas, beliefs, and emotions.* On this vivid life journey, you have to learn to recognize your emotional and mental state. That awareness will give you the tools you need to pull yourself out when you find yourself slipping into a negative spiral. Disappointment or frustration often creeps in when things are not coming together as fast or smoothly as you had hoped—*whether it is about money, relationships, or simply feeling like progress is slow.*

We often let mental issues stop us in our tracks. The usual suspects are fear in all its forms, frustration because you know things could be better, or disappointment when they are not. You need to figure out what makes you feel helpless or upset. To do that, you have to understand how your brain and your mind interact.

If you want to undergo a major transformation to step into a vision you may have held onto for decades, it will demand a new version of you. Know that your brain will fight you every step of the way, trying to pull you back to old ways of thinking and doing. The brain is a survival tool—it manages your bodily functions, interprets external information, and keeps you safe. Its primary job is protection, which means it often perceives change as a threat, even when that change is necessary for growth. This protective mechanism can result in mental blocks, confusion, or disorganization, especially in moments of stress or when difficult memories resurface. While these responses are designed to shield you, they can also hold you back if left unchecked.

In contrast, your mind operates in the realm of your thoughts, emotions, and beliefs. It is intangible, housing your attitudes and aspirations. When the brain resists change, the mind must step in to challenge those fears and refocus your energy. This is where you can take control by identifying and addressing negative patterns. Pay attention to what occupies your mental space. Are unproductive thoughts or external influences taking over? Recognizing and clearing these distractions is essential to staying aligned with your vision. If you do not understand this process, you will be an easy mark for those inner villains.

When you allow ideas, the voices and actions of people, or negative situations to take up space in your head rent-free, you are not in control. Marketers know this—they try to carve out space in your brain by introducing new ideas and creating grooves that occupy your thoughts. Politicians do it. They tell stories that take hold, whether they are true or not. You have to be aware of what is taking control of your mind.

When you feel confused, disorganized, and cannot articulate your thoughts, it is a sign of mental clutter. We also experience mental blocks—moments when we cannot recall information or perform tasks due to stress or suppressed memories. These blocks show up to protect us, but if we do not recognize them, they can sabotage instead.

Mental clutter—those moments when you feel overwhelmed or stuck—is a sign that your internal systems are misaligned. By understanding the difference between your brain's instinctual resistance and your mind's capacity to reframe and overcome, you will truly be the hero of your vivid life story. Awareness will be your superpower. It will allow you to reclaim the narrative, turning blocks into breakthroughs.

Acting On What You Believe

You need to get your head in the game because your thinking impacts your believing. You cannot have vision if you do not believe in the future. The key to your vivid life is finding a vision that imposes discipline on you. First and foremost, I am speaking of mental discipline.

I have this unique ability to see big, giant, colossal, ridiculously huge projects—*equal parts artist and architect*. I gain an intense level of satisfaction as a big picture is defined and comes to life for others to understand and embrace. I am a visionary. If there is a problem to be solved, I am like a moth to a flame. I have to try to solve it. I am a visionary. Whenever I am asked, *"What are you working on?"* I have to giggle before I respond because I realize that if I tell the truth, most of the time it will sound preposterous. Imagine the comfort I derived from the definition of the word *"visionary."*

ADJECTIVE: given to or characterized by fanciful, not presently workable, or unpractical ideas, views, or schemes; NOUN: a person of unusually keen foresight; a person who is given to audacious, highly speculative, or impractical ideas or schemes; dreamer – Dictionary.com

Ambiguity is my friend. Possibility and Purpose are her cousins. Even if you cannot agree with those sentiments for yourself wholeheartedly, let me state again that the Bible clearly says, *"Where there is no vision, the people perish…"* So, that tells me that if I am not happy with any area of life, it is because I do not have a vision for better. I like the part of the definition that says *"not presently workable."* Your vision, by its very nature, will not be workable this very moment. That is why it is a vision. It is a big picture.

Vision gives you what you need to endure any test, trial, or trauma, and in every life, there will be many. You can say, *"I want a better job,"* but you have to define what *"better"* is. It is that blurry picture way out on the horizon. I am imagining those dream sequences in movies. They are glowing and idealistic. Think of your impractical, blurry vision that way. Habakkuk 2: 2 says, *"Write the vision, and make it plain."* Making it plain, *or vivid*, is bringing it into focus.

When your vision is tested—*and it will be*—you will learn something about perseverance. To pass the test, you will have to make a very important decision. Will you fold under the pressure, or will you rise to the occasion? Your vision will help you make decisions. It will determine what you say yes to, and it will make the no's much easier. Your focus will become keen, and you will be unstoppable. You are the one who can make your impractical schemes a reality. Every one of us needs something to strive for, something on the horizon. You cannot afford to sit around waiting for that *"something"* to come to you. You must take action on what you believe. You are the hero *becoming* whatever the vision needs.

You Have To Become The Prophet Of Your Own Future

Living your vivid life at play requires more than just imagination—it demands that you become the prophet of your own future, someone who does not just dream but sees, declares, and shapes what is to come. A prophet sees with clarity, speaks with intention, and acts with purpose. To live a life of purpose, you have to *see prophetically* by beginning with the end in mind and then *speak prophetically* to bring that vision to life. So, what are you seeing and saying about your future? What is the vision for your life, your business, your family, and your relationships? What *"end"* are you envisioning?

Prophets in ancient times were more than mere fortune-tellers. They were visionaries who saw beyond the present, understood the potential of the future, and boldly spoke it into reality. A prophet does not just observe—they interpret, clarify, and declare, empowering others to see what they see. Similarly, your role in your life is to see the end clearly, to visualize your goals with intensity, and to speak with conviction about what you see. By declaring your future, you turn possibility into reality.

Your future is not a distant, impossible dream. It is a destination you can navigate toward every day. Living life at play involves actively creating that destination. Growth, then, is about declaring your desired destination and becoming to reach it. That is not a type-o. I will repeat it. Growth is about declaring your desired destination and *becoming* to reach it. Starting with the end in mind gives you both direction and intention, and when you speak what you see, you lay down stepping stones for action. What you declare about your future builds it. The Living Bible translation of Habakkuk 2: 2 says, *"Write my answer on a billboard, large and clear, so that anyone can read it at a glance and rush to tell the others."* The next time you are speeding down a busy highway, take not of the billboards and how vivid they have to be for you to get the message with the radio blaring and the kids laughing as you go by. Think of seeing and saying your vision prophetically like that. As the prophet of your own future, you must refine your vision until it is vivid. Write, rewrite, and adjust until the picture is unmistakably clear. With each word, the image in your mind's eye sharpens, and as your vision becomes vivid, you will naturally start to speak it, act on it, and see it unfold. When you declare what you see, you are fueling your vision, giving it the energy to become real.

The Work of Becoming

One of the biggest successes of my professional life came to an abrupt and brutal end. In spite of that trauma, I was facing an exciting transition into client projects with people who valued the depth of my capabilities, doing work that fed me creatively while making a real difference, and finally getting compensated for the value I bring. It felt like my career, aspirations, and life's work were all amounting to a beautiful becoming.

My husband was finishing out the year in San Francisco taking care of his mother. So, I spent New Year's Eve through January 2nd with a circle of dear, enterprising friends. We prayed for each other and shared our visions for the future. I had a sense that in the coming year I would use it all—*all of my obsessions and loves, all of my experience and dreams, all that I had to offer*.

I had a longing for spiritual insight, and somehow, during this seeking season, the YouTube algorithm presented a 3-part series by Randy Feldschau. Pastor Randy began by explaining the difference between the Hebraic calendar followed by the Jewish people versus the Gregorian calendar used by the rest of us. Basically, he shared that it was 5783 on the Jewish calendar, and he described it as the year of the camels—a time of provision for purpose.

My Expectation Was Ignited

He went on to speak of repayment and reward for destiny, activation in divine order, and told me (yes, me personally—at least in my head) to drink from the well of the vision of life. (He had me at *"vision."*) He used words like *"blessing"* and *"elevation with ease"* and *"year of possibilities."* (As I review the notes in my Flip Book now, I have to admit I am getting triggered by what feels like betrayal. Pastor Randy set me up.)

I could see the future unfolding. I am immediately transported back to those hours before the clock struck midnight. My mind is fast forwarding through the giant Post-It pad papers covering the walls, the giddy excitement of sharing ideas over breakfast with a sister in revelation, and the confirmation of it all by Pastor Randy's camels. Only in hindsight, I can now hear the disarming scratch of a needle being abruptly pulled across a vinyl record as I see myself walking into my impending reality of that year just eight days later. Oblivious.

Honored to Step Into a Period of Service

My husband needed to come home to Atlanta, but I knew he would be worried about his mother. So, I offered to switch places. The plan was that I would be with Mom for two months in San Francisco. I assumed we would just take turns, and this was mine.

After living alone for thirty-three years, she was not willing to leave the city she had known for over 80 years and the place she had called home for seven decades. Being the military brat that I am and an entrepreneur who worked remotely before it was a global thing, it was an easy decision. However, I was clueless about what 24-hour caregiving looked like.

I was so honored that my husband trusted me with his mother, but I had never spent time with senior citizens, never been a caregiver, and never been in San Francisco longer than a week. I was in a new city living in my husband's childhood bedroom unaware of the isolation that was lurking. I remember describing to one of my friends that it felt like I hit a wall in every direction I turned. She responded, *"That's because there's nowhere to go but up."*

And the Understatement Award of the Year Goes To

Remember those client projects I mentioned? Not one of them came through. My bank accounts emptied. No return phone calls. No final signed contracts. No income. No prospects. Those two months came and went as my husband had to deal with mounting pressures at home. My stay was extended indefinitely. Suffice it to say that my world was going through a personal pandemic. My usual coping mechanisms were not working. *"Up"* was actually the only way I could go. God wanted to get my attention and jerk the proverbial slack out by fencing me in with no opportunity to stray. I could only look up.

I even hit a milestone. My 60th birthday was spent alone and marked by a devastating feeling that I had nothing to show for it. My mental state had deteriorated despite every feeble attempt to fight. That was the bottom, but

CHAPTER 7: **Living Life At Play**

thankfully, I had those dear friends I mentioned. A simple, honest text that I felt like a failure with nothing to show for my sixty years yielded an immediate and effective response. They sent me music, spoke life, and scheduled an emergency Zoom meeting to throw in some cackles. (That is how my husband describes our full body laughter.)

The short story is that I was able to embrace my new home away from home, examine myself, and learn some vital lessons that I desperately needed. Otherwise, I could not be ready to receive what the camels were bringing. I finally understood the cycle I had fallen into. There were decades spent giving myself fully to everyone else's projects. I believed more in theirs than I did in my own. Remember the *"abrupt and brutal end"* of my successful project. I believe that happened because I poured everything into someone else's vision while neglecting mine. My first waking thought on the first day of the following year was, *"failure to launch."*

Failure to launch is a psychological term that describes the inability of a young adult to establish their independence and embrace the transition from adolescence to adulthood. The concept can be applied to the challenges you and I face with becoming everything we were designed to be. Failure to launch hinders our progress, growth, and impact.

Time to Use It All

One thing I am known for is not quitting. I do not give up on ideas. Instead, I have been collecting and building and refreshing and repeating that process. I have gained understanding and some wisdom, but I have not launched fully. I failed to launch my poetry collection, album, and devotional in 2004, Vivid Magazine and Baudacity in 2005, Flip Productivity™ System in 2011, my international dollhouse miniature exhibition in 2013, and Vivid Academy nonprofit in 2020. I did not give up on them though.

Now I see that my camels have been bearing the weight like champions, and they are bringing it all back with everything I need. Their arrival was dependent on my ability to unburden myself of the doubt, ignorance, and fear of disappointment that was brewing under the surface. The gift of my caregiving season is that I left one year hopeful for the provision the camels were bringing and entered the next confident that I was ready to receive them.

I knew nothing would be lost or wasted, and it will be right on time. That entire year brought exactly what I needed to step into my identity, influence, and impact. Finally, I am on the launching pad.

The Dignity & Divinity of Work

You are made in the image of your Creator, with the power to create and cultivate your environment like Adam in the garden. Living your life at play is about finding your purpose in the dignity and divinity of work. One day, I stumbled upon *The Butler* on Netflix, a film I had seen for the first time a decade earlier.

As I re-watched it, the movie hit me in a way it had not before. Social justice movements and my own journey with my DNA brought up so many emotions. My identity is more Nigerian and more British and Irish than I realized, and seeing all of that on paper was a powerful, personal reckoning. Watching *The Butler* in that context, the phrase that stuck with me was *"the dignity and divinity of work."*

As the film unfolded, showing the life of a White House butler who served eight presidents, it was striking to watch how he and others were treated in their work. Yet, there was a beauty in watching them grow more skilled in their labor. It got me thinking about how valuable work is—the ability to apply yourself to something and be rewarded not just with money but with a sense of accomplishment, satisfaction, and the ability to chart your own destiny.

This legacy of work is a gift from God Himself. It is not something any human can control. There is dignity and divinity in the work we are called to do, not just the jobs we hold for a paycheck but the work we are purposed and gifted to do. As I reflected on this, I came across a purpose grid I had created, which outlines the trajectory of finding purpose. What I have realized is that we cannot find our purpose outside of the work we are doing. The two are inextricably linked.

Finding your purpose is not something that just happens one day. It is a process. Just like faith and works go hand in hand, you can believe something about yourself, but you have to do the work to learn what it truly means. It is in that work that your purpose reveals itself. I want to help you find your purpose

CHAPTER 7: **Living Life At Play**

in the dignity and divinity of work. You have heard people talk about their life's work or career, but it is deeper than that. In our society, we tend to define success by jobs, titles, and salaries. I want to challenge you to see it another way. Your purpose is not just about solving your problems or the problems of those around you—it is about the work you are uniquely designed to do, the work that feeds your spirit, not just your bank account.

Purpose does not always reveal itself immediately, and sometimes we have to work our way into it. At other times, we are forced to make a change, when we are pushed into the unknown. As painful as those moments are, they often propel us into something better, something more aligned with our purpose (like my caregiving). When it feels unbearable, that is when your strength rises up, and you find what you need to keep going. You start to realize that even in the challenges, there is something beautiful emerging—a better life, a deeper understanding of yourself, and a clearer path to your purpose.

This does not happen with just a job. It is made possible by work you are graced to do. It is about the gift you have been given and how you use it to make a difference. When you find that work, everything starts to fall into place. It is not always about money at first, but the fulfillment and joy you get from doing the work you were meant to do. Through vision, communication, study, talent, and discipline, you will discover what drives you and what makes your work meaningful. The money follows. The truth is, we are all responsible for our actions and our work. We may not control everything that happens around us, but we have the power to shape our own lives through the work we do and the purpose we pursue. So, let's embrace that power and step into the purposeful work that we were created to do.

Five Keys to Finding Your Purpose

Finding your purpose can feel elusive and even daunting. With so many distractions, expectations, and demands, it is easy to miss or lose sight of what truly drives you. We live in a world that often pushes us toward production over fulfillment, leaving us with a sense of emptiness rather than purpose. Many people spend years or even a lifetime searching for a sense of meaning, only to feel that something important is missing.

Purpose is more than just doing what you enjoy—it is about aligning your actions with a deeper calling. It is the sense of direction that keeps you grounded and energized, even in difficult times. That said, defining purpose is challenging because it requires some inside work that is at times brutal. This will demand courage to face what you find. Then, you must be honest about the role you have played in the best and worst of it. All of this will tempt you to just give in, so I want to provide you with these five keys. Rather than looking outward for answers, these keys encourage you to look within to define how you are intended to show up in the world.

1. Vision | Defining Your Life's Direction

Vision is the foundation of purpose. When you lack a vision, life begins to feel unfocused and aimless. This is what it means to *"perish"*—to move without purpose, to lose motivation, and to drift through life without a guiding force. Vision opens your eyes to possibilities beyond the present, offering a compelling picture of what is possible. It empowers you to look past what *is* to imagine what *could be*, setting the stage for intentional and meaningful action.

Take a moment to consider areas in your life where you feel stuck, uninspired, or unfulfilled. Reflect on past seasons when things seemed off course—how might things have been different if you had a guiding vision? Without this sense of purpose, it is easy to fall into routines that lack energy and direction. Vision is what gives purpose its wings, steering your decisions and infusing every action with meaning.

2. Communication | Sharing Your Purpose Opens Doors

Purpose is not something to keep to yourself. It is meant to be shared. When you communicate your gifts and goals, you open doors for connection and collaboration. Communication is how you articulate your vision, allowing others to understand and support your journey. By sharing your purpose, you attract opportunities that align with it. Think of communication as your bridge to the world—it is through your voice, writing, or daily actions that others see who you are and what you have to offer. This act of sharing draws people, resources, and ideas that can help you fulfill your purpose.

3. Study | The Difference Between Self-Exploration and Self-Absorption

Self-exploration is an essential component of purpose, but there is a fine line between studying yourself to grow and becoming self-absorbed. Self-exploration focuses on understanding your strengths, values, and passions so you can serve in ways that matter. It is not about obsessing over yourself, but about gaining insights that help you work toward your purpose. This intentional practice of examining your habits, emotions, and talents helps you become clear on what drives you and where you need growth. Make time to study what genuinely excites you and identify how you can bring those passions to life in service to do greater works.

4. Talent | Using Your Gifts to Serve Unexpectedly

Your talents are clues to your purpose. The abilities you possess, often without even realizing their full value, are not just for your own benefit—they are tools to serve others. When you share your talents, you may find unexpected ways they can touch lives, provide solutions, or inspire others. Developing your talents is a way to honor the unique skills you have been given and opens avenues for making a meaningful contribution. As you refine these gifts, you will see how they fit into the larger context of your purpose. Purpose-driven work aligns your talents with the needs of others.

5. Discipline | The Pain and Power of Staying the Course

Discipline is the backbone of purposeful living. While it can be challenging—*often uncomfortable or even painful*—discipline is what transforms good intentions into achievements. This key to purpose requires commitment, especially when you face obstacles, fatigue, or self-doubt. Discipline is like a muscle that gets stronger through use, enabling you to keep going despite hard times. Think of it as the commitment to show up every day, no matter how difficult it may be.

Each of these five keys plays a critical role in defining your purpose. Vision gives you direction, communication creates opportunities, study brings self-awareness, talent enables service, and discipline fuels persistence. When you cultivate each of these, you are on your way to a life at play. (I'm a poet, and I know it.)

Purpose is Liberating

Living with purpose brings a profound sense of freedom. It liberates you from the need to conform to others' expectations, from fears of inadequacy, and from the endless pursuit of approval. Purpose clarifies who you are and what you are meant to do, empowering you to break free from the limitations of doubt, indecision, and comparison. When you are anchored in your purpose, you can live with confidence and joy, knowing that your path is unique and divinely designed.

To live liberated is to wake up each day with a sense of clarity and intention. You are not bound by the constraints of external validation or temporary measures of success. Rather, you are free to walk your path, make bold decisions, and pursue what truly resonates with your spirit. Living liberated means you are able to express yourself fully and embrace the gifts you have without shrinking back or dimming your light.

When you live liberated:

You experience an inner peace that comes from knowing you are on the right path, even when challenges arise. You no longer question every decision or wonder if you are good enough, because you have aligned your life with a purpose that fills your soul.

You feel a deep sense of joy in the work you do, the relationships you build, and the life you are creating. This joy is not conditional on external success but springs from the knowledge that you are fulfilling your purpose.

You are unafraid to take risks and step outside your comfort zone, knowing that growth and fulfillment lie in embracing new opportunities. You see setbacks as learning opportunities, not failures.

You have a resilient mindset, seeing each obstacle as a stepping stone rather than a barrier. Even in the face of adversity, your purpose keeps you moving forward with determination and grace.

You live with authenticity, unburdened by the need to prove yourself. You show up as your true self, unapologetically and wholeheartedly, embracing your unique design.

Say Goodbye to Constraints

Without purpose, life can feel like a series of disconnected events, leading to frustration, confusion, and a lack of fulfillment. When we live without purpose, we become susceptible to the pull of other people's opinions, and we are often driven by fear instead of freedom.

When you live constrained:

You feel weighed down by others' expectations, always trying to fit into roles or meet standards that do not resonate with who you truly are. Your decisions are influenced by what you think others want, rather than what you feel called to do.

There is a persistent sense of dissatisfaction, as if something is missing. Even when you achieve success by conventional standards, it does not feel meaningful or fulfilling.

Fear holds you back from taking bold steps or exploring new directions, because the risk of failure feels overwhelming. Instead of viewing challenges as opportunities, you see them as threats to your comfort or security.

Your actions lack consistency or direction, often feeling reactive rather than proactive. Without a guiding purpose, it is easy to drift, trying various things but never fully committing to any path.

You struggle with self-doubt, constantly questioning whether you are good enough or comparing yourself to others. That only leaves you feeling small and incapable of reaching your full potential.

Say goodbye to a life defined by limitations and the constant pull of external expectations. You have been liberated. You do not have to be weighed down by what others think or be held captive by fear. Say goodbye to living on someone else's terms. Purpose gives you permission to live boldly, embrace your own standards, and create a life that reflects who you were meant to be.

The Exhilaration of Alignment: Living True to Your Design

When you begin living with purpose and embracing the liberation that comes from knowing who you are, what you have to offer, and your life's work, something incredible happens. You get in alignment. Alignment is the feeling that arises when your values, actions, and direction all converge. This is when life stops being a struggle against the current and starts feeling like a natural, powerful flow toward something great.

Alignment brings with it a sense of ease and excitement. Imagine a child at play, fully immersed in what they are doing—whether building, imagining, or exploring. They are completely present, lost in the moment. Similarly, when you are aligned with your purpose, work and play merge, and tasks that once seemed tedious or overwhelming begin to feel fulfilling and enjoyable. It is no longer about simply getting things done. It is about engaging with each activity in a way that fuels your spirit and brings out the best of your abilities.

Being aligned is a return to authenticity—a shedding of outsider expectations and a commitment to walk in the rhythm that is yours alone. Just as a well-tuned instrument produces beautiful music when played in harmony, so too does your life become a symphony when you live in alignment. Decisions become easier, boundaries clearer, and there is a quiet confidence in knowing that you are right where you are meant to be.

Moving from being purposed and liberated to living aligned is a journey of trust. Trust in yourself, in the process, and in the One who designed you. It is letting go of the need to have everything lined up and instead allowing your true self to emerge, guiding you toward the next step, and welcoming what unfolds. When you live aligned, you will feel that childlike wonder we talked about returning.

The Freedom of Yielding: Embracing Life's Flow

After discovering purpose, experiencing liberation, and finding alignment, there is a final, transformative component of living life at play—*learning to live yielded*. Yielding might seem counterintuitive in a world that often glorifies control, hustle, and certainty, but true freedom is found when you can release the need to control every outcome. Living yielded is about trusting the path that is unfolding, embracing your vivid life's natural flow, and allowing yourself to be led by something greater than your own plans.

To yield is not to surrender passively. It is to lean into life with openness and faith, like a child who trusts that they are cared for, even when they do not know all the answers. This childlike quality—*an ability to trust, wonder, and release*—is what allows us to yield gracefully. In this state, we begin to see life as an adventure, full of twists and turns that can surprise us, deepen our experience, and guide us to places we might never have chosen but ultimately need to go.

When you live yielded, you are free to experience life with less resistance. Living yield is a *"yes"* mindset, even when you do not fully understand. You have embraced your purpose, felt the liberation of authenticity, and aligned with your core values. Now, yielding becomes a willing surrender to what life has in store—trusting that each step, each moment, will carry you closer to becoming the person you are meant to be.

This kind of surrender is freeing because it removes the weight of constantly needing to *"do"* and instead allows you to *"be."* Yielding does not mean giving up. It means letting go of striving, choosing to flow with life rather than forcing your own way. Jesus called it learning the unforced rhythms of grace.[19] In doing so, you reclaim the wonder and openness of childhood, seeing every day as an opportunity to learn, grow, and be surprised by the unfolding story that is uniquely yours to tell.

Living yielded is the final step in a life that is purposed, liberated, and aligned—a life that flows naturally with peace and wonder, fully embracing each moment with gratitude and trust.

Transformation Is a Team Sport

Have you heard the saying, *"It takes a village?"* Since we are social beings, true transformation requires the support and synergy of others who walk alongside you. Your gifts are for others, and their gifts are for you. That is just how God designed us. Your vivid life cannot fully flourish in isolation. Community is the foundation of growth—a place where we not only learn but become, build, connect, and get involved in the lives of others.

Community provides a unique space where learning and personal growth are multiplied by shared experiences. In our lives, just as in entrepreneurship, there are lessons that books or YouTube videos alone cannot teach. These lessons come alive when we engage in community, drawing on the knowledge, strengths, and perspectives of others. Seek out transformative spaces for visionaries, leaders, and change-makers who want to make an impact in the world.

You will learn more with others. Growth requires study and practice, but it is also about translating knowledge into meaningful action. You do not want to only gather more information. You want to learn how to apply it in ways that align with your vision. Each member of your community—whether coaches, mentors, or fellow learners—contributes insights that turn ideas into reality, helping you to continually refine your approach and stay on task, focused on your goals.

You need coaching and mentoring. Every top performer relies on trusted mentors and coaches who offer guidance from their own experience. Having people who have walked the path (or are taking the trip with you) makes it clearer, faster, and more effective. You need instructors who are entrepreneurs and innovators themselves, not just academics, who bring their life's work into teaching and mentorship, ensuring you are not only inspired but equipped for real-world challenges.

You need resources and support. Growth requires resources—whether knowledge, finances, or practical tools. Community emphasizes sharing these resources effectively, allowing each member to plant seeds that lead to greater influence and positive change. Everything starts with a seed, and in community, you will find the support needed for nurturing and growth.

Community helps you uncover and develop your talents and calling. You need a place where you are not only fulfilling a role—you are discovering the unique way you are meant to serve, lead, and create change. This process of becoming is deeply personal, and it requires the support and encouragement that a strong community can provide.

It Is Not What You Know, But Who

Living a vivid life at play is challenging, and it is not something you should have to do alone. Being connected to the right people can make all the difference. Community offers encouragement, accountability, and inspiration, helping each member stay true to their purpose while pursuing their unique path.

Community provides the experiences, environment, exposure, examples, and encouragement to stay on course. In a supportive environment, transformation happens organically. Community is a space for action and growth—a place for new experiences. It is where faith meets works, where you will develop the skills you need to turn your thoughts into action. Members at all stages can give and receive encouragement, share wisdom, and celebrate each other's successes and provide support when it is desperately needed, knowing they are part of a team that genuinely cares.

In Community, you will be exposed to new ideas and perspectives that can shape your approach to life and business. You will have the opportunity to connect with builders at every stage, learning from those who have walked similar paths. This exposure helps to open doors you may not have considered, allowing you to explore options that resonate with your purpose and apply what works best for you.

One of the greatest benefits of Community is finding examples of people who have navigated similar challenges and can offer guidance and inspiration. You can learn from others' experiences. These relationships can shorten your learning curve, helping you progress faster and with greater confidence. Best of all, in moments of struggle, the community's support provides the motivation and reassurance you need to keep moving forward as you build something extraordinary together—one vision, one connection, and one breakthrough at a time.

Just like your days on the playground, Community is not without its pitfalls. People be peopling, as they say, and they will break your heart, disappoint you, hurt your feelings, and more. Be careful because you might be the perpetrator yourself. So, proceed with an abundance of grace to kiss and makeup.

In this chapter, you have journeyed back to a time of curiosity, boundless imagination, and fearless exploration—the essence of childlike wonder. Reclaiming this perspective is not just a nostalgic exercise. It is an essential step toward living a life at play: purposed, liberated, aligned, and yielded to everything life has in store.

I have shown you that you are a masterpiece, intricately designed with unique attributes, strengths, and callings. Recognizing yourself as God's handiwork allows you to step fully into who you are meant to be, confidently and unapologetically. Each element of your design serves a purpose, and embracing that purpose brings the freedom to walk your own path without fear of judgment or the need to conform.

You are invited to live aligned with the rhythm, the soundtrack that God has produced just for you. This alignment with your values, vision, and purpose creates a natural flow where each step becomes more meaningful, where work and play converge, and where the journey itself is as rewarding as the destination. When you live aligned, you are embracing life with an open heart, just as a child approaches each day—*ready to be surprised, ready to explore, and ready to grow.*

Finally, living yielded means trusting the process, letting go of the need for control, and embracing the unexpected twists and turns. This mindset allows you to fully surrender, experiencing life as an adventure that is rich with possibility. Living life at play means embracing every moment with wonder, trust, and gratitude, secure in the freedom that comes from knowing you are right where you are headed in the right direction.

In rediscovering your childlike wonder, you are not just returning to who you once were. You are stepping into the fullness of who you were created to become. Let this chapter be your call to action—*to live purposed, liberated, aligned, and yielded*—as you make your life vivid.

CHAPTER 7: **Living Life At Play**

Re-VIEW [PLAY Key Points Summary]

- Resist conformity, and rediscover the strength to stand out, embrace your true self, and resist the urge to blend in just to gain approval.
- Reflect on the unguarded curiosity, joy, and creativity you had as a child to reclaim your childlike wonder.
- Create your PLAYBook, a sort of personal brand guide and creative space to record and explore your dreams, values, and milestones.
- Recognize that you are God's masterpiece, crafted intentionally like brushstrokes in a painting, so embrace your divine design.
- Your existence is a marvel of intricate biological design and divine intention, so celebrate that you are *"fearfully and wonderfully made."*
- Understand your psychology to counteract negative thoughts, stay focused, and step fully into your potential.
- Vision is not enough. You must act on what you believe.
- You have to become the prophet of your own future—seeing and declaring the future you imagine.
- Purpose honors the dignity and divinity of work.
- Say goodbye to constraints by finding purpose that liberates you to live boldly on your own terms.
- Alignment is the exhilarating feeling that arises when your values, actions, and direction all converge.
- Yielding is the art of letting go of control, trusting in a greater plan, and embracing life's unexpected turns.

Your A.C.T. List [Action to Complete This Task]

☐ What were you like as a child?

_____
_____
_____
_____

☐ When did you learn it was not safe to speak your mind, share your ideas, or stand out?

_____
_____
_____
_____

☐ What would play look like for you now?

_____
_____
_____
_____

CHAPTER 7: **Living Life At Play**

Resources

Worksheets

- Purpose Grid
- Flip Productivity™ Play Worksheet Fillable PDF

Vivid Academy Community

The space where visionaries, leaders, and change makers create the future they imagine. Visit vivid.academy.

PLAYBook Toolkit

Visit playbook.gwenwitherspoon.com or scan the QR code to download worksheets, get video links, and other resources.

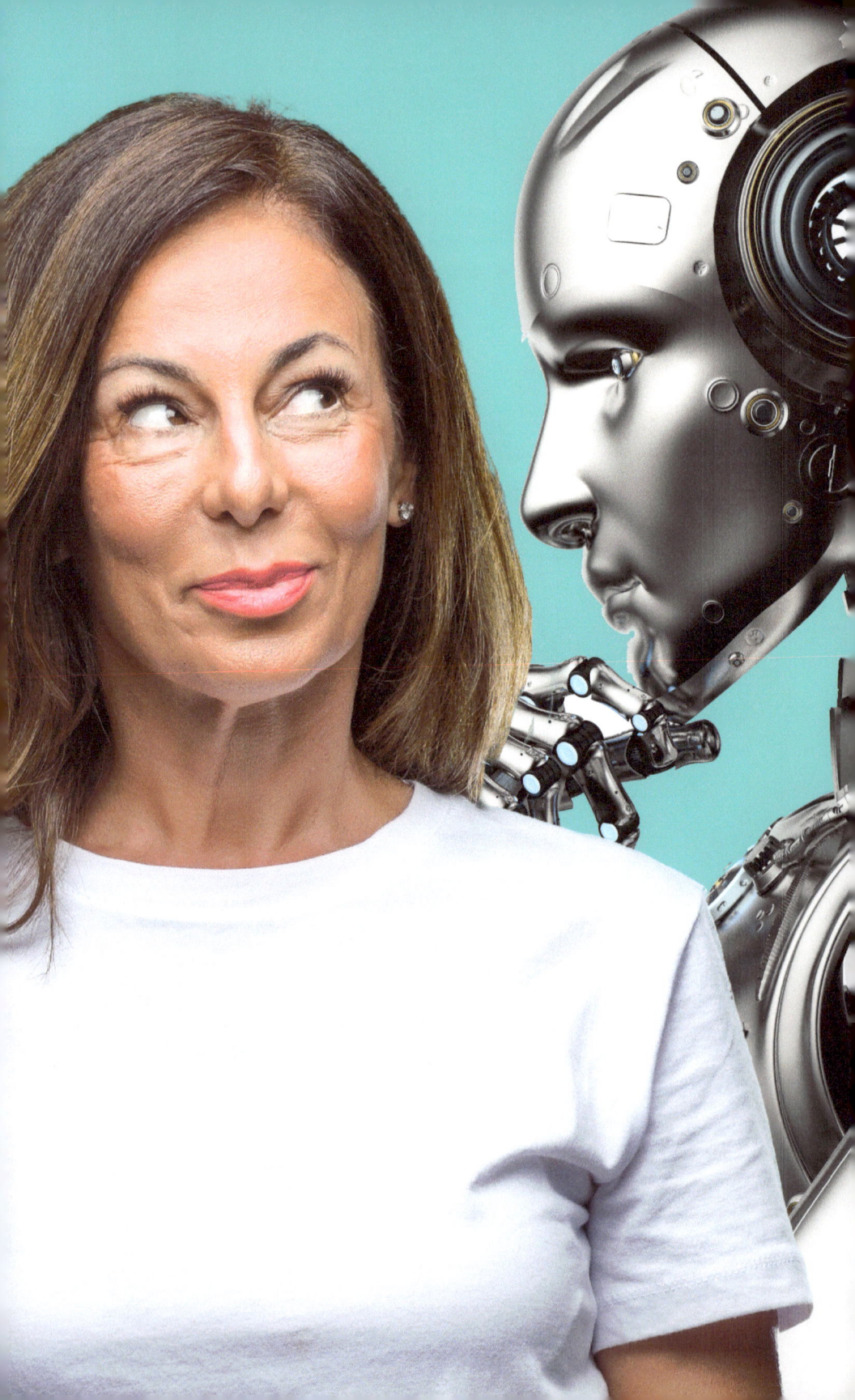

CHAPTER EIGHT • CONCLUSION

No More Hiding Your Light & Playing Small
[TIME TO GLOW UP, SHOW UP, & GROW UP]

Are you ready to stop making excuses?

Remember that I said you are God's masterpiece? You needed to know that so you could stand up a little taller, but now I have to inform you that masterpieces are not hidden away or forgotten—they are created to captivate and inspire. They are placed in the spotlight, celebrated for their splendor and ability to convey powerful messages. In the same way, you are not a product of chance or circumstance. You were crafted to be seen, valued, and shared. **You are here to glow up**, to shine with purpose, and to bring out the *"God-colors"* in the world. Your identity is a living, breathing testament to God's love, meant to brighten the lives around you and reflect His light in profound ways. Your glow up is when you introduce yourself to the world as your magnificent self.

This is your notification to stop holding back and to step fully into the vibrant, purposeful life you were designed for. When you show up, it should be with confidence, finding your unforced rhythm, and embracing the life you were called to live. You bring something irreplaceable to the table—a distinct set of gifts, talents, and abilities that no one else can replicate. Your role in this world is vital, and your presence is essential. **Show up fully and unapologetically, knowing that what you have to offer is necessary.** You show up prepared to be the difference maker because you are, you have, and you know enough.

That is not all. Your life's work is not just about signing up for the race.

Make Your Life Vivid

Completing your life's work will require you to grow up. That means welcoming the challenges, enduring through the pain, and *becoming*. Growing up means embracing the discomfort that comes with transformation, knowing that each trial refines and strengthens you. Growth is about becoming who God destined you to be—a powerful force for good, a kingdom builder, and an ambassador of change. Every step is preparation for the incredible impact you are meant to make. To truly live a vivid life is to use your identity, influence, and impact to finish well.

Making your life vivid is about perseverance—*finishing what you start with determination and faith*. The process begins with writing it on paper, on your mind, and on your heart. The vision you have been given is about crossing the finish line and fulfilling your highest calling. The equipment you need is embedded in who you are and activated by what you do—the equipment you need to finish. Finishing is not the opposite of failure—*it is the fulfillment of your calling.*

The Art, Science, & Psychology of a Vivid Life

Making your life vivid means embracing the artistry of your creation. Builders of all kinds use their imagination to create something beautiful, something that inspires others. Your life is a canvas, and every choice you make adds to the masterpiece you are creating. Whether you are building a business, crafting a story, or solving problems, never forget that your creativity is a divine gift. Imagination is a divine spark—use it to illuminate your path and inspire others along the way.

A vivid life also requires structure to complete your assignment. The science behind your success involves experimenting with ideas, testing your strategies, and learning from failure. Just as scientists observe the world, builders use data, strategies, and systems to make their vivid lives possible. Planning is your tool to enable what you are building—to ensure that your efforts produce lasting results.

Lastly, living a vivid life is about mastering your inside world for transformation. Your thoughts, emotions, and habits are the building blocks of your future. By mastering your mindset and developing discipline, you can face any challenge with hope, resilience, and the confidence to succeed. It is

CHAPTER 8: Conclusion

not just about dreaming big, it is about cultivating the mental and emotional strength to bring those dreams to life.

Prepare Your Soundtrack

The soundtrack in a movie plays a crucial role in shaping the atmosphere and enhancing the storytelling. It is more than just background music—it sets the emotional tone of a scene, evokes feelings in the audience, and adds layers of meaning to the narrative. Music can establish the setting, emphasize key moments, and even foreshadow future events. It helps with pacing, providing rhythm and continuity, and it can even offer insights into a character's emotional journey. A well-composed soundtrack deepens the audience's connection to the story, making the film more immersive and impactful. You need a soundtrack, a playlist to set the tone for each day, to get you through difficult moments, and reset your outlook when you need answers. What music makes you feel powerful, reminds you who you are, or declares your future condition?

I am reminded of when as a single parent, I took a leap of faith to replace the Subaru station wagon whose right door had rusted shut. When I picked my son up from school, he had to enter through the back seat and crawl into the passenger side. There was no money set aside, but I decided to just go look. I walked the lot and found a used car that was much nicer than the ones I was used to. Though it required a real investment, I asked for a test drive. I took one of my favorite CDs with me. I drove familiar streets and took note of how it felt with every turn while listening. I left the lot with that same CD playing in my Subaru, and in the days that followed, that soundtrack kept me focused on the future I had imagined. Faith was the only currency I had at the time. So, I took action based on what I saw for myself and my son. I do not remember how it all worked out, but I will never forget the moment I was driving down the Alaska Highway at night and my son pressing the button for his electric seat to recline fully, and hearing him say, *"God is so good,"* while that same CD played.

No More Excuses

I tell that story because we really did not have the money, but I used what I did have. We are in a moment of unparalleled opportunity in history. Artificial

Intelligence has removed barriers that once limited reach and influence, creating pathways for us to leverage our gifts, share our stories, and make an impact across the globe. Today, technology makes it possible to amplify who you are, expand what you have to offer, and bring your life's work to those who need it most. This is your time to break free from excuses—AI has given you tools to share your voice with clarity and confidence, to create with purpose, and to reach the world in ways that were unimaginable just a few years ago.

Yet, if you are like many, certain pain points may still hold you back. Perhaps you feel overwhelmed by the process of defining and communicating your personal brand. Maybe the fear of misusing AI technology, or a belief that you lack the skills, prevents you from exploring the possibilities. AI can be a powerful partner, providing not only a technological boost but also clarity, efficiency, and guidance that empowers you to move beyond limitations.

Defining Your Personal Brand With AI

AI offers a unique set of tools to help you understand and communicate who you are, so your personal brand reflects your authentic self. With AI-powered personality assessments, you can gain valuable insights into your strengths, values, and communication style. Imagine using these insights to refine your brand and discover what resonates most deeply with others. AI can help you clarify your unique message and build a brand that truly reflects who you are.

Visual consistency is another key aspect of brand identity, and AI-powered design platforms can support you in this area. Tools like AI-driven design suggestions enable you to experiment with colors, layouts, and imagery that align with your message, even if you are not a designer. Your visual presence becomes a coherent, compelling representation of your brand that builds recognition and connection with those who encounter it.

As a creative and brand strategist, I know that there is more to building your personal brand than a few keystrokes and instantly generated images. However, even I cannot deny the power that artificial intelligence puts in the hands of every person with an idea. It is mind-blowing. If nothing else, AI can

CHAPTER 8: **Conclusion**

help you work through what you have in your head and provide you with the basics you need to make progress at lightning speed. If you can ask questions, have a conversation, or just talk, AI can absolutely help you define your personal brand.

Amplify What You Have to Offer

Creating and sharing valuable content is essential, and AI can help you do it with ease and efficiency. AI-driven content creation tools assist in generating ideas, drafting blog posts, and writing social media content. Imagine having a tool that supports you in articulating your thoughts, allowing you to focus on refining your message rather than struggling to start from scratch. With AI, you can bring your ideas to life quickly and effectively.

AI also allows you to repurpose and distribute content across various platforms, reaching more people in different ways. For instance, a podcast episode can be transcribed, summarized, and turned into an article or a social media post.

Additionally, AI-driven automation tools streamline the distribution process, helping you schedule and optimize posts so your content is shared strategically. By removing the burden of managing these logistical details, AI frees you to focus on the creative and purposeful aspects of your work.

Telling Your Vivid Life Story with Global Reach

Your story deserves to be heard, and AI offers powerful tools to ensure it resonates far and wide. Through advanced translation tools AI enables you to communicate with people across linguistic boundaries, making your message accessible to a diverse audience. Imagine the impact of connecting with someone halfway around the world, sharing your story and insights in their native language. AI gives you the ability to meet people where they are, adapting your message so that it reaches those who need it most, no matter where they are in the world.

Video is a powerful way to tell your story, and AI-driven tools make it easier than ever to create, edit, and distribute high-quality video content. Platforms allow you to add captions, edit clips, and even include voiceovers, giving you the tools to produce polished videos that capture your message. With video, your audience can see your passion, hear your voice, and connect with you on a deeper level, enhancing the emotional impact of your story.

AI also transforms how you approach targeted outreach. By using AI-powered advertising platforms like Google Ads or Facebook Ads, you can connect with specific audiences who are most likely to resonate with your story. AI's targeting capabilities allow you to tailor your message, ensuring it reaches those who need it most, even if they are on the opposite side of the world.

Without going into too much more detail, I need you to understand the power of what is available to you. I earned my graphic design degree two years after Apple released the Macintosh computer. In those days, to be a freelance designer, I had to spend literally thousands dollars just to get a laser printer. You could not publish a book and print copies on demand. There were no mobile phones that you could use to record yourself, and there was certainly no YouTube that allowed you to create your own channel. With all of that, AI can shrink timeframes, information gaps, and budget limitations to make you more effective faster.

The Partner You Have Been Waiting For

AI is not just a tool. It is a partner that helps you overcome the challenges that may have stopped you in the past. It provides structure and clarity, especially when you feel overwhelmed by the sheer scale of building a personal brand or expanding your influence. AI's ability to streamline processes can ease the burden of complex tasks, giving you more time to focus on what truly matters: the substance of your message and the impact of your work.

For many, a major barrier is the fear of not having the technical know-how, but AI is designed to be intuitive and accessible, removing the need for advanced technical skills. With the support of AI, you can step out of your comfort zone and embrace new possibilities without the fear of failure. Think of AI as an amplifier for your talents—a partner that enhances your strengths

CHAPTER 8: **Conclusion**

and makes your work more impactful.

It is also common to feel skeptical about AI, worrying that it might detract from the authenticity of your message. However, AI is not here to replace your voice. It is here to enhance it. You are still the driving force behind your message, your creativity, and your vision. AI simply provides the tools to help you express these elements more effectively, reaching a wider audience and maximizing your potential impact.

AI As a Partner in Your Purpose

Using AI is a way to ensure that you steward your gifts wisely, maximizing the reach and impact of your message. In a world where technology and faith can intersect, AI becomes a tool that empowers you to live out your purpose more fully. It enables you to finish well, to persevere in sharing your story with a consistency and clarity that leaves a lasting legacy.

AI does not replace you—*it amplifies you*. It provides the framework, insight, and reach necessary to fulfill your highest calling. As you harness these tools, remember that your voice, your message, and your story are powerful. You have everything you need to impact the world, to shine your light, and to make your vision vivid. No more hiding, no more playing small—it is time to leverage all that is available to you, without excuse, and step boldly into the vivid life you were created to live. With AI as a partner, there truly are no more excuses. The opportunity to share who you are, what you have to offer, and your life's work is greater than ever. So, glow up, show up, and grow up to tell your vivid life story.

Come Out of Hiding

With AI as a partner, there is no reason to keep your light hidden. You have the opportunity to glow up—*to use the gifts you have been given and illuminate the world around you*. You can show up in a world that needs your ideas, your wisdom, and your voice. You can grow up by refining your message and taking your responsibility to take it seriously. It is time to break free from the limitations of fear, self-doubt, and hesitation. AI has unlocked the door to a future where your potential can be fully realized, where your message can reach those who need it most, and where you can make an impact that matters. No more excuses—take a deep dive into your vivid life, and let AI support you as you embrace the opportunities in front of you.

Finishing Well

It is easy to give up, to quit, when the finish line is in sight. Exhaustion sets in, doubts creep up, and the idea of stopping feels like a justified reward. After all, you have come a long way, and no one would blame you. Quitting may bring temporary relief, but finishing offers a profound and lasting sense of accomplishment. You overcame every setback. You endured the pain. You fought through fatigue. You did the work.

Starting something new is exciting and often easy. It is the follow-through—the grit to persevere when it is hard. That is how you finish. Finishing well requires patience, focus, and resilience. It is about not letting obstacles, fatigue, or even your own comfort rob you of the satisfaction that comes from completing what you set out to do.

Think about areas in your life where you have stopped just short of the finish line. What would it have meant to push through, to see it through to the end? Finishing well is not just about checking off a task—it is about proving to yourself that you can embrace the process, rise above challenges, and make it to the end.

This commitment to finishing extends into everything you do. Whether you are pursuing personal growth goals, building relationships, or completing professional milestones, the ability to finish well signals integrity, fortitude, and strength. It is about consistently giving your best effort, not just when it is easy, but especially when it is hard. There is a special kind of power in finishing. It transforms the effort and time you have invested into something meaningful,. When you finish well, you prove that your vision and goals are worth the struggle. You affirm that the journey is no just about starting—it is about who you become by seeing it through.

Finishing well is not just about reaching the end. It is about the growth, determination, and discipline you gain along the way. It is about showing up for yourself, staying true to your purpose, and giving everything you have got to make your life and work matter. So, when you feel like giving up, remind yourself that finishing is not just an option—it is the only way to truly honor the effort you have made and the potential you hold.

Who You Are [Glow Up]

"You are here to be light, bringing out the God-colors in the world...If I make you light-bearers, you don't think I'm going to hide you under a bucket, do you? I'm putting you on a light stand. Now that I've put you there on a hilltop, on a light stand—shine!" – Matthew 5: 14-15 The Message

Living your vivid life means that you have made peace with your past, you are content in your present, and eagerly pursuing your future. You have embraced the art of creation, the science of execution, and the psychology of growth. Ready to allow the shadows of your soul to be illuminated, you willingly endure scrutiny because you are determined to bear fruit. This commitment enables you to shine your light, to stay inspired and focused, and appreciate the gift of God imparted to you.

Who lights up the world? Who do we celebrate? Those whose identity, influence, and impact are known and experienced. They have mastered their talent, time, and treasure. We look up to them. They inspire us.

However, you are here to use your gifts to become the light you are destined to be. We need your ideas, your personality, and your genius to shine. Yep. Yours. No carbon copies, no business as usual–only exactly what God intended for such a time as this. What problem were you born to solve? Your Glow Up includes an invitation and a dare. You are invited to become more than you have ever imagined and all that God has designed, and I dare you to *be* the light.

What You Have to Offer [Show Up]

"Each of you should use whatever gift you have received to serve others, as faithful stewards of God's grace in its various forms." – 1 Peter 4: 10 NIV

To *"show up"* is more than merely occupying space—it is about bringing the fullness of who you are to every moment, every conversation, and every opportunity. Showing up means embracing the unique gifts, talents, and insights you have been given and offering them to the world with courage and conviction. It is about realizing that the world does not just need people to be present. It needs people to be engaged, involved, and actively contributing their God-given gifts to make a difference.

Imagine your life as a divine appointment. Every interaction, every moment of influence, is a sacred opportunity to show up with intention, to be fully engaged, and to give what you have been uniquely equipped to offer. Showing up is about choosing courage over comfort, purpose over passivity, and impact over invisibility. The world needs the authentic version of you, not the masked or diminished version. When you show up with everything you have, you honor God's design in you, and you give others permission to do the same.

Consider what it would mean if you held back—if you allowed fear, doubt, or comparison to keep you from showing up fully. The world would be deprived of the insights, compassion, and creativity that only you can bring. Showing up is an act of faith and surrender, an acknowledgment that you are enough, that you have been given enough, and that you know enough to make a difference. God has placed a unique purpose within you. Showing up means saying, *"Yes,"* to that purpose and sinking yourself into it with everything you have.

Your Life's Work [Grow Up]

"Consider it a sheer gift, friends, when tests and challenges come at you from all sides. You know that under pressure, your faith-life is forced into the open and shows its true colors. So don't try to get out of anything prematurely. Let it do its work so you become mature and well-developed, not deficient in any way." – James 1: 2-4 The Message

Growing up in the context of a vivid life is not about merely aging or gaining experience. It is about embracing the trials, challenges, and growth opportunities that shape you into who you are meant to become. Growth is the process of refining and of stepping into a more mature, grounded, and impactful version of yourself. Growing up is the work of transformation—allowing God to shape you through each experience, each hardship, and each moment of grace.

CHAPTER 8: Conclusion

Every challenge, every disappointment, every success, and every failure is a part of your growth. God uses each of these moments to mold you, to strengthen your faith, and to deepen your resilience. Growing up means embracing the discomfort of change, welcoming the stretching that comes with new challenges, and surrendering to the process of transformation. It is understanding that each trial is a gift, a step closer to becoming the person you were destined to be.

To truly live a vivid life, you must be willing to grow—*steadily, intentionally, and without shortcuts*. This journey requires maturity, commitment, and the courage to endure. Growth is not always easy, and it rarely comes without sacrifice. Each step, each lesson, and each struggle refines you, preparing you to fulfill the purpose for which you were created. Growing up means persevering through the difficulties and trusting that God is shaping you into a powerful force for good.

In Summary

It is time to embrace the call to live boldly and without reservation. You have been invited to shake off the confines of conformity and step into a life that is unapologetically yours. You have been challenged to see yourself not as a reflection of others but as a powerful original, designed to make an impact in ways only you can. Living a vivid life means creating a future with a vision that ignites the deepest parts of who you are.

Your identity, influence, and impact are gifts that carry the potential to shape the world around you. You were made to be a solution—an answer to the challenges and needs that you encounter. The vivid life calls you to transform dreams into reality, not just for personal success, but for the cause of goodness. Each decision, every effort, and all of your talents converge to help you build a legacy.

Purposeful living is fueled by intentional habits that shape your days, align your actions, and deepen your impact. Every habit you cultivate is a step toward becoming the person you were meant to be. As you recapture that childlike wonder, embracing the joy, freedom, and playfulness of life, you reconnect with a spirit that refuses to be limited by fear or the status quo. You were born to approach each day as an adventure, with a heart open to new

Make Your Life Vivid

possibilities and a soul ready to grow and explore.

Now, as you step forward, it is time to glow up—shine brightly through all of who you are, unhindered by fear or doubt. Show up fully, bringing your whole self to the table, offering the world your gifts, perspectives, and talents. Finally, grow up by taking responsibility for your life's work, pressing on with resilience and courage as you pursue your highest calling.

Are you ready to stop making excuses? Your vivid life awaits—a *life where you no longer hold back, no longer hide, and no longer play small*. You have everything you need. The world needs your vision, your story, and your courage. Now is your time to make your life vivid. When you do, you will no longer live by default—*you will live by design*. So, I challenge you to take the lessons from this guide and make them your own. Step into your light, embrace your calling, and become the person you were meant to be. The world needs you, and only you can deliver the message God has written on your heart. Now is the time to make your life vivid. Now is the time to glow up, show up, and grow up.

Thank you for allowing me to be your coach. Our relationship does not have to end here. **Make Your Life Vivid** is a guide that you can refer back to over and over, so come back and *"see me"* often. The resources in the PLAYBook Toolkit will be updated from time-to-time, but I know that the do-it-yourself route only works for a moment. Eventually, you will need help to get beyond what you can do alone. Whether that is group or one-on-one coaching or services to build your personal brand, I got you. Let's finish well, *together*.

CHAPTER 8: **Conclusion**

Re-VIEW [Conclusion Key Points Summary]

- **Who You Are:** You are here to be light.
- **Glow Up:** Masterpieces are meant to inspire and captivate, and you are designed to shine brightly, fully embracing your unique identity to bring light and color to the world.
- **What You Have to Offer:** Use your gifts to serve others.
- **Show Up:** Showing up means bringing the fullness of who you are, your gifts, and your talents to every moment, choosing courage over comfort.
- **Your Life's Work:** Let your faith life be forced into the open to do its work, becoming mature and well-developed.
- **Grow Up:** Growth is about embracing challenges, enduring discomfort, and allowing transformation to shape you into the person you are destined to become.
- **Finish Well:** Finishing is not about starting strong but about persevering through difficulties to complete your life's work.
- **Make Your Life Vivid:** Step into a life designed with purpose, creativity, and courage, refusing to hide, shrink, or settle for less than what you were designed for.
- Every top performer needs a coach, mentors, and community.

Your A.C.T. List [Action to Complete This Task]

☐ GLOW UP! What gift will you use to shine?

_____
_____
_____

☐ SHOW UP! How will you stop hiding?

_____
_____
_____

☐ GROW UP! What is your life's work?

_____
_____
_____

☐ Name the top 5 songs for your vivid life soundtrack.

_____
_____
_____
_____

CHAPTER 8: Conclusion

Resources

Artificial Intelligence

There are countless AI tools available, with more released every day. So, instead of providing suggestions here, scan the QR Code below with your mobile phone, and look for them in the PLAYBook Toolkit.

Vivid Branding Accelerator

What do you want to create? Answer five questions, and turn your answers into LIVE AI prompts to define your idea in real-time. From there, you will have the foundation for completing any project–a book, pitch deck, funding proposal, course, blog, social media campaign, email marketing, and more. Whatever you have heard about artificial intelligence, it could be the tool you need to destroy every barrier preventing your progress.

PLAYBook Toolkit

Visit playbook.gwenwitherspoon.com or scan the QR code to download worksheets, get video links, and other resources.

Brands By Gwen

   AdamRed.agency
1. Vivid Magazine
2. Baudacity.com[21]
3. WomenOfRumble.com
4. MissDorothysGarden.com
5. MyWaterCounts.com
6. GwendolynFaye.com[22]

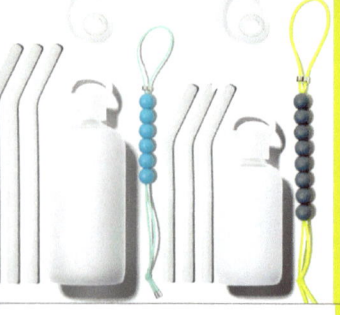

Let's Talk.

< Scan to Schedule

About the Author

Gwen Witherspoon
VIVID LIFE INFLUENCER

Gwen helps visionary leaders write their vivid life stories so they can live life at play–*effectively doing, while delightfully being*–instead of missing out on all the goodness available to them by becoming a copy of someone else.

As an artist and entrepreneur, she uses art, technology, and music to define your identity, influence, and impact using her V.I.V.I.D.™ Model. Gwen is the one you come to when you are ready to make your weaknesses irrelevant, find your rhythm, and receive everything God has destined for you.

Builders rely on her to interpret that God-breathed idea they feel destined to complete.

Faith leaders look to her to make their brand stories vivid and create experiences that change the world without sacrificing their values and callings.

Nonprofit Founders count on her to develop comprehensive brand strategies without getting overwhelmed by what they don't know or don't have.

References

[1] The Holy Bible, Psalm 139: 14, New International Version.

[2] The Holy Bible, Genesis 1: 26 New International Version.

[3] The Holy Bible, James 1: 17 New International Version.

[4] The Holy Bible, Jeremiah 29: 11 New International Version.

[5] Strong's Concordance Number: H2896, Hebrew: (tov), meaning *"good, beautiful, pleasant, agreeable, beneficial."*

[6] The Holy Bible, Proverbs 29: 18 New King James Version.

[7] The Holy Bible, Proverbs 29: 18 The Message.

[8] The Holy Bible, Acts 9: 1-19 King James Version.

[9] The Holy Bible, Romans 10: 17 New International Version.

[10] The Holy Bible, Romans 10: 17 New International Version.

[11] The Holy Bible, Ephesians 1: 4 New International Version.

[12] The Holy Bible, Jeremiah 1: 5 New International Version.

[13] The Holy Bible, Matthew 5: 13 New International Version.

[14] The Holy Bible, Matthew 5: 14 New International Version.

[15] The Holy Bible, Esther 4: 4 New International Version.

[16] The Holy Bible, Psalm 2: 8 New Living Translation.

[17] The Holy Bible, John 14: 12 New International Version.

[18] The Holy Bible, Genesis 11: 6 King James Version.

[19] The Holy Bible, Matthew 11: 28-30 The Message.

[20] Marje, *"Are You Afraid of the Dark?"* A Love Invasion, 2000, lyrics excerpt.

[21] PHOTO CREDIT: Ron Witherspoon Photography.

[22] PHOTO CREDIT: Tony Tyus for 40 Plus Wonders.

www.ingramcontent.com/pod-product-compliance
Lightning Source LLC
Chambersburg PA
CBHW041629220426
43665CB00001B/2